ELATIONSHIP

SELLING

The Fine Art of Consultative Sales

Atul Uchil, PhD

Outskirts Press, Inc.
Denver, Colorado

Table Of Contents

Acknowledgements

I dedicate this book to my wife Patricia for her unconditional support through the good and the not-so-good times and for being my inspiration, my rock.

I also have to thank Patricia for giving me my kids Lindsey (my daughter) and Cory (my son). Lindsey and Cory bring me joy and meaning and lest I forget trials and tribulations. However, they always light up my life.

My parents have been an inspiration my entire life. They are the well from which I draw my strength. They instilled in me discipline, honesty, integrity and perseverance. Mom and Dad, I love you.

Major Byron Love (USAF – Ret.), your friendship and loyalty knows no bounds. You have extended your support and friendship to me; always encouraging me to go that one extra step. You are truly a man of honor. I also need to mention an extra word of thanks to you for convincing me to write this book.

I thank Lieutenant Colonel Ken Beutel (US Marine Corps - Ret.) and Lieutenant Colonel Deb

Beutel (US Marine Corps - Ret.) for their friendship and support over the years. They are both true patriots and both of them are recipients of the Legion of Merit medal. They are also the nicest and kindest people you will ever meet. These are people who will do anything for their friends. Patricia and I consider ourselves blessed to have you as friends. Ken & Deb, it is truly an honor to know you.

Phil Carrai has provided me with mentorship and guidance for more than half my career. Phil stood by me as a mentor and a friend through the years. He ensured my survival in trying times by providing me with that one extra word of advice and encouragement to keep me hanging on. Phil you will always have my heartfelt gratitude and loyalty.

Lieutenant Commander Jimmy Lewis (US Navy – Ret.), I thank you for being a good friend and a solid, down-to-earth sounding board for my ideas. I value and treasure your friendship and your counsel.

I thank Lieutenant Colonel Thomas Stuckey Jr. (US Marine Corps - Ret.) for his guidance, advice and eagle eyes. It is a distinct pleasure and honor to call you my friend.

Commander John Potts, (US Coast Guard – Ret.), I thank you for the years of guidance, advice and wisdom. All that I have achieved as a staff officer in the USCGA, I can directly or indirectly attribute to you.

Bill, Karen, Ray and Nancy Ashton, you have treated me as part of your family for the past two decades. You always accepted me for who I am through all the vicissitudes of my life. I feel proud to be associated with your family.

Linda Yoo, I thank you for your loyal and steadfast friendship over the years. Your counsel has been an invaluable asset. You are a true friend.

I cannot help but mention Kent (Big-M) Morgan, the wise old man. He is not that old but definitely wise beyond his years. His calm stoic attitude and approach has saved my bacon more than once.

No book is ever completed without the help of many people whose friendship, advice and help are critical to the completion of the project.

To all of you that I have not explicitly mentioned here, I extend my gratitude for your help and my apologies for not having your name here.

SPECIAL NOTE: I cannot thank my wife Patricia enough for putting her considerable talents as an artist and muralist at my disposal in order to conceptualize and paint the cover image for this book.

Introduction

I have not sold a single thing in my career that has spanned twenty-four years to date. When I say anything, this includes hardware, software, services, commodities, etc.

Let me caveat the above with the following statement.

"I am NOT counting the temporary part-time job of a sales person that I had while I was attending college as a part of my twenty-four year career."

I do not plan to sell anything to anyone as long as I continue in my career. If you have not screamed rip-off and thrown the book away yet, you are probably asking yourself, "What business has someone who claims not to have sold anything writing a book on relationship selling?"

Let me tell you why. I have honestly lost track of the revenue that I have generated over the past twenty-four years. However, I have been credited with a generating a little over two hundred million dollars in revenue during the course of the past five years.

<u>YES! - I STILL CLAIM THAT I HAVE NEVER SOLD.</u>

Let me explain. I do not sell products, services or commodities. I just establish strong relationships with my clients and achieve the coveted status of a trusted advisor. My clients elect to buy services and/or products from me. I never try to sell them.

I know that this sounds deceptively simple. Almost as if I just sit around and wait for things to happen. As this book will explain, establishing and maintaining trusted client relationships without trying to sell them anything, requires a lot of patience and a constant struggle against the temptation to start selling.

There have been many times in my career where I have felt that all I had to do was nudge the client just a little bit and I would have a large sale. However, I have held myself back, knowing that once I pushed the sale, my relationship with that particular client would change from that of a trusted advisor to that of a transactional sales person.

This is the very situation that I have strived to avoid thus far in my career.

Some of you are probably wondering, if this approach works or if it just a bunch of bull. Let me unequivocally assure you that it has worked for me.

Here is an example. I have acknowledged Retired Major Byron Love of the US Air Force prominently in this book.

Over the past several years, whenever we got together, Byron has reminded me of an incident that took place at a US Department of Defense Joint Command. I cannot mention the name of the joint command in this book. Further, he has tried several times to convince me to write a book highlighting this incident.

Let me tell you about the incident in question. At that time, I was working as the Senior Vice President of Operations for a beltway bandit. "Beltway Bandit" is a term referring to the multitudes of small and midsized business organizations located in Washington, DC, Northern Virginia and Suburban Maryland.

These companies make their living by securing and delivering on contracts for the Federal Civilian Agencies and Department of Defense (DoD).

During my tenure at this beltway bandit, I chose to maintain personal interactions with a few select clients. Because of my position within the organization, the sales and professional services divisions reported to me. I had several well qualified Program Managers and Sales Persons working for me.

However, I had cultivated strong trusted advisor relationships with these clients over several years. I did not see the need to forego them just because I had a fancy title.

One such client was Colonel John Wright at the Joint Command mentioned earlier. The organization that I worked for was in the process of delivering a collaboration services technology solution to this Joint Command.

Collaboration Services were on the bleeding edge of technology at the time. So much so, that there were only about twenty to twenty-five systems-architects/programmers in the country that had truly mastered this technology. Two of these programmers (David Smith and Eugene Edwards) worked for my organization.

I have to make one or two more points to lay the groundwork. Then I will get on with elaborating the incident that I mentioned.

We had completed Phase 1 of the engagement. Phase 2 was about two or three weeks shy of completion. The Government had not yet funded Phase 3.

The Federal Government typically funds projects one phase at a time or one fiscal year at a time depending on the type of contract.

Anyway, David & Eugene (the programmers) came to me on a Wednesday morning and informed me that a rival company had offered them twenty-five thousand dollars as a sign-on bonus. They asked me to match it or else.

This is where they made a critical mistake. I wish that they would have come to me and said that they had done market research and concluded that their skills were worth twenty-five thousand dollars more.

I would have had HR investigate and given them the raise simply because they were integral to the success of a client engagement that generated over ten million dollars in revenue annually.

However, since they gave me an ultimatum, I wished them well and accepted their verbal resignation on the spot.

I counsel you that if you ever find yourself in the situation where you feel your skills are worth more that you are being paid, reason with you bosses using facts, figures and your performance. Do not ever give your boss an ultimatum. Even if you give your boss an ultimatum and he or she accepts, you have only achieved a temporary victory. You may have won the battle but you have actually lost the war. You just soured your relationship with your boss and your employer organization. This will come back to haunt you.

Getting back to the incident ---

Now that both my systems-architects had resigned, I had the unpleasant duty of informing the client. I called Colonel Wright's office and requested an urgent meeting. The meeting was set for Thursday morning at 9:00 AM. I arrived about twenty minutes early for the meeting and ran into Major Byron Love.

I usually visited the Joint Command every other Tuesday, so Byron was surprised to see me onsite on a Thursday. I explained the situation to him. I told him that I was there to inform the Colonel that the completion of Phase 2 would be delayed by about two weeks and that the two main programmers had resigned.

I remember Byron's first reaction just as if it was yesterday.

He said, "Man, I like you and your program team members a lot."

"But, the Colonel is going to fire your ass and terminate your company's contract when he hears this."

Byron made this statement prior to my meeting with Colonel Wright. Since he was supporting Colonel Wright and was intimately involved with the project, I asked Byron to accompany me to the Colonel's office.

Byron and I went in to the meet the Colonel at 9:00 AM. I am not going to reveal what happened in the meeting just yet. However, here are Byron's post-meeting comments.

As soon as we came out of the Colonel's office, Byron said, "Man, I do not understand what just happened. You went in there, gave the Colonel a lot of bad news and walked out with an extension on the Phase 2 completion date and signed funding for Phase 3."

The Phase 3 funding was approximately five million dollars.

Over the years, Byron and I have become trusted friends. I see Byron once every two or three months and every time we meet, he says, "I was there and I still do not understand what happened."

"I was so sure that you would get fired when you walked into that meeting."

"Instead, you walked out with a five million dollar contract. You need to write a book about this."

Well Byron, I am finally writing the book thanks to your repeated urging.

ADDITIONAL THOUGHTS: *I wrote the text above this prior to this paragraph when I began writing the book. Now that I have completed this book, I feel the need to add the following text to the introduction.*

When I initially started planning this book, I envisioned it to be a precisely structured treatise. It was going to have well-structured chapters with surgically precise (in other words dry and drab) content. However, after I started writing, it seems that my passion for this subject has gotten the better of me. If you have read any of my prior books, you know that I only write books on topics that I am passionate about.

It appears that I have traded some of the structure for more informative real-life experiences. Many years of accumulated information, experience and knowledge, has escaped the confines of my mind and driven my fingers to type words in some form of spontaneous overflow of powerful thoughts and feelings.

I have decided to write the gist of the above message on the back cover of this book and caution the reader of the following.

If you are looking for a well-structured book with information delivered in precise format, this may not be the best book for you. However, if you are looking for an abundance of relevant information interspersed with over almost a quarter century of real-life experiences both good and bad narrated with a lot of passion and caring, you will find this book stimulating and insightful.

You decide!

Chapter One
Buying Versus Being Sold

- People like to buy.
- People hate being sold or being forced to buy.
- People buy from people that they like and trust.

Everyone has encountered the above three statements. You have heard them either verbatim or by means of different words that convey the same or similar meaning.

All people go through a distinctive buying process regardless of whether they are buying groceries, buying consumer goods for their home or making large purchases for their corporations.

- The first stage in this process is to perceive need.
- The second stage is to research alternatives.
- The third stage is to make the purchase (decision).
- The fourth stage is to perform post-purchase analysis.

There is no defined timeframe and/or set of tasks that need to occur in each of these stages.

Sometimes this process is very short. For example, an individual is not going to perform weeks of research on what type lettuce they plan to buy.

Sometimes this process is very long and drawn out. For example, a corporate executive will almost always perform a significant amount of research before buying a five million dollar CRM system for his or her corporation.

Some of you are probably saying yeah right! I do not go through that process every time I buy. What if I was going out to dinner? I am not thinking through four stages. I just go out and eat.

Well it is my turn to say, "No! You do not just go out and eat." You go through the process either consciously or subconsciously. Here is how it works.

Perceive Need: I am hungry. There is nothing in my refrigerator. I need to go out and eat.

Research Alternatives: What do I feel like eating today? - Chinese, Mexican, Steak, Italian, Fast food or Pizza.

My clothes have been fitting a little too snug this past few weeks, may be I should avoid fast food.

I like Chinese food, but I had it earlier this week. The Italian restaurant is eight miles away. I can just walk to the Mexican restaurant. It is on the next block. The food is not bad and it is not too pricey either.

Make the Purchase (Decision): I guess am going

to have Mexican food for dinner tonight.

Post-Purchase analysis: That burrito is sitting in my stomach like a rock and I feel heartburn coming on. Maybe I should have driven to the Italian place or just stayed in and ordered a pizza. A pizza would have been just as cheap. The Italian place was pricey. However, I would not be suffering heartburn now. OR

That was the best burrito I ever had and I am full. I am glad that I decided to eat Mexican food tonight.

Therefore, it seems apparent that we go through the four stages of buying regardless of what we are buying.

Let us examine these four stages from a corporate perspective. I do not think anyone out there is reading this book with the intent of understanding his or her decision process when choosing a restaurant. At least I hope not.

Stage1 – Perceive Need: The individual decision maker, group of decision makers or corporate management perceives a need.

This perceived need might sometimes be an urgent or critical need, like that perceived because of an existing or imminent crisis.

For example, someone hacked into our systems, our competitor already has it, government regulation dictates it, etc.

At other times, the perceived need may be less urgent.

For example, the existing accounting system is becoming outdated so we would like to update our accounting system soon, we should get more health

3

insurance benefits for our employees, etc.

Regardless of the urgency, when the corporation identifies a need, they usually begin analyzing alternatives. This leads us to:

Stage2 – Research Alternatives: The analysis and research of alternatives is typically (not always) a documented process within most organizations. Regardless of whether it is formal or informal, written or unwritten, it exists.

For example, one organization might have a purchase evaluation team that analyses all alternatives and prepares written reports for upper management to decide. In other cases, it might just be one individual, a mid-level or senior manager, who gets multiple quotes before deciding.

Either way, involvement at this stage is very important for you - the sales professional. If you already have a trusted relationship with the sole decision maker, the sole decision maker's superiors, the organization, or some member of the organization who has a reasonable amount of credibility as a strong influencer, you can rest assured that you (your company) will be one of the factors considered in the analysis of alternatives.

If you do not have the trusted relationship, it is almost too late to try to develop it at this stage. I am not saying that it is impossible to do, as I have seen it done successfully even at this late stage. I am just stating that it is an uphill battle.

I am also stressing the importance of

establishing relationships with clients, regardless of whether you think they have a current need for your services or products.

You can rarely predict with a reasonable degree of accuracy when an organization might perceive need.

Stage 3 – Make the Purchase (Decision): The organization issues a purchase order or bill of sale and makes the purchase.

Stage 4 – Post-Purchase Analysis: This is another critical stage in the process. Your relationships with the stakeholders can make or break your deal at this stage. This applies regardless of who makes the purchase or how the purchase was made.

There is always at least one (typically more that one) naysayer within every organization. This person or these persons will question the decision and raise doubts about the effectiveness and performance capabilities of the solution that was purchased. The questions usually raised are:

- ◆ Did we really need it?
- ◆ Did we perform enough research on the alternatives available in the market?
- ◆ Did we get a good deal?

If the person or persons that made the decision were in the buying mode, they will defend the decision as if their life depended on it.

Conversely, if the person or persons that made

the decision felt like they were being sold or being pressured to buy, they will defend the decision half-heartedly at best.

In addition, I have observed the following two scenarios repeatedly over the past two decades.

Scenario 1: The sales professional and/or onsite program manager has a trusted relationship with the stakeholders. The solution performs with only ninety percent of the capabilities that the client purchased.

The client still points to the ninety percent, claims victory and success, and then showers the sales professional and/or project team with praise.

Scenario 2: The sales professional and onsite program manager does not have a trusted relationship with the stakeholders. The solution performs with ninety-nine percent of the capabilities that were sold.

The client still points to the one percent and blames the sales professional and/or program manager for the failure. Alternatively, the client begrudgingly accepts that the system performs to specifications.

This brings us back a full circle to the first three statements in this chapter.

♦ People like to buy.
♦ People hate being sold or being forced to buy.
♦ People buy from people that like and trust.

Let us examine the rationale behind these statements in detail.

Why do people like to buy? Buying gives people a feeling of satisfaction, a feeling of accomplishment or a feeling of power.

I have spoken with many directors, purchasing managers, Vice Presidents, CEOs and Government acquisition personnel etc. and all of them make the same set of statements in somewhat different words.

- ◆ I have a million dollar purchasing budget. (Purchasing manager, director)
- ◆ I decide who buys what in this company or division. (CEO, Vice President)
- ◆ No one can buy a pencil in this company without my approval. (CEO, Vice President, Purchasing Manager, Director)
- ◆ I have level-3 acquisition authority. (Government personnel)

If you read between the lines or in this case listen between the sentences, what are they really saying?

SHHH! Listen carefully. I personally hear the following:

- ◆ I am powerful.
- ◆ I have authority.
- ◆ I deserve respect.
- ◆ If you want to do business with this organization, you will acknowledge me.

7

Just think of yourself for a moment. Think of how you would feel when you walked into the electronics store pointed to the XYZ brand plasma flat screen TV and told the sales person.

"I will take one of those in a box."

I think you would feel good.

Alternatively, consider this scenario. You walk into a car dealership. You proceed to stand by the most expensive sports car they have, (let us say Corvette – "always buy American" is my personal motto), and look at it.

The sales person walks over and you tell him or her, "I will take that Corvette. I do not need financing."

"I will pay by check. Just call my bank and verify funds. Then have the paperwork ready for me to sign and the car washed, detailed, and waiting out front."

How would that make you feel? I am willing to state that you feel satisfied, happy, and powerful or some combination of these feelings.

Therefore, I guess you will agree with me when I say people like to buy.

Now think back to the Corvette scenario. Let us assume that you live in Cleveland, Ohio. When you tell the sales person that you would like to buy the Corvette, the following occurs.

Instead of obliging and selling you the Corvette, the sales person gives you a very logical argument on why you should not buy the Corvette but buy an SUV instead. Let us say a Hummer or Hum-V (whatever they are calling it these days).

He makes a very logical and persuasive argument about why the SUV will serve you better in the snow. He also explains how the Hummer will still be status symbol just like the Corvette.

He further explains to you how if you bought the Corvette you could only drive it for eight months of the year, reasoning that it is potentially unsafe to drive a sports car on the snowy Cleveland streets in winter.

Let us also assume that the sales person's argument is logical and strong enough to convince you. You accept that the sales person's points are well made and valid. You give in to the sales person's recommendation (persuasion) and buy the Hummer instead of the Corvette.

How do you think you would you feel after the purchase? Would you feel powerful, would you feel satisfied, would you feel happy?

Alternatively, do you think you would feel dissatisfied or feel uneasy like your experience is somehow incomplete?

Well, guess what, there is no surprise here. Everyone I spoke to agrees that he or she would categorize this experience with negative feelings. The negative feelings can be attributed to an adverse mental reaction to being sold or being forced to buy.

I know that some of you are thinking the following, "I am a business consultant or I am a management consultant."

"If I cannot ever tell the client what they need even when I know it is good for them, how can I ever be a trusted advisor and give them advice?"

BINGO! You hit the nail on the head! How do you give the client advice without making them feel like you are selling to them?

That is the key skill involved in being a trusted advisor. As a management consultant or a business consultant, you should be able to advise and help the client without forcing your opinion on them. You should be able to give the client objective advice and help them make the decision.

DO NOT make the decision for the client and then try to convince them to accept the decision.

MOST IMPORTANTLY, do not make the client feel like they are being lectured, chastised, forced, or cornered into the decision. We will deal with the aspect of providing trusted advice later in this book.

Let us get back to the topic at hand. Point number three on the list. People buy from people they like and trust. Here is why. Every one who is buying something significant is doing one of two things.

♦ They are putting out their hard earned money. Or
♦ They are putting their reputation and/or job on the line.

What do you think happens to the Vice

President who spends five million dollars of company funds and purchases a CRM system that does not perform with the expected (required) functionality?

Sure, the company might sue the seller and/or not pay them, etc. Nevertheless, that Vice President just made what we can call a CLM (career-limiting move). If he or she is not demoted or terminated outright, he or she is definitely not going to be promoted anytime in the near future.

Therefore, when someone is planning to spend corporate funds, they want to feel assured that the person they are buying from will deliver on promises and do right by them.

This is where genuineness, sincerity and honesty play an integral role. Assuming that you have not exaggerated the capabilities of your organization, the product your organization delivers will meet and/or exceed your client's expectations.

This will result in your client trusting you more. Consequently, this will result in them buying more from you. This cycle will repeat as long as you do not lose the client's trust by lying or being dishonest.

If something unexpected happens that affects the quality and/or schedule of your delivery to the client, make certain that you inform them as soon as you know.

Do not try to hide things, sugar coat things, spin things etc. The client may get mad at you for the time being when you deliver bad news. However, as long as you have dealt with them honestly, they will come back to you with more business.

I am not implying that you can keep messing up on delivery quality or schedule and still expect to keep the client's business.

If your organization is repeatedly missing quality or schedule, you may have a much bigger problem. Either you are not being honest about your organization's capability or you have an incompetent organization.

If it is the latter, I recommend that you find another job. If it is the former, reevaluate your understanding of your organization's delivery capability to be more realistic when setting client expectations.

Chapter Two

Types of Relationships

As a sales professional, there are really only two types of interactions that you can have with your clients. They are:

♦ Transactional and
♦ Trusted advisor

Before I delve into the two types of interactions, let me define what I mean when I say sales professional.

If you ask people at large, what comes to mind when they hear the words 'sales professional', almost everyone replies sales person, inside sales, outside sales, sales manager etc. Rarely does anyone mention client-site engineers, client-site programmers, project managers, program managers, etc.

I have been mainly associated with the professional services divisions of many large and small companies throughout my career. Somehow, I have always ended up playing the revenue generation role in all of these corporations.

The only time in my career that I held a sales related title was when I worked as a part time sales person at Radio Shack to augment the meager funds that I received from the University to compensate for my Research Assistantship.

In my first year as a sales person for RadioShack, I received the 'One Hundred Thousand Club' award. This was my first and only sales award. I have kept it to this day.

It is a pewter mug with my name and the words '$100,000 Club' engraved on it.

I was young. I thought the award was cool. Now days, I prefer to receive a percentage of the revenue as my award. I will buy my own pewter mug if I need one.

I am talking about the early eighties here folks. In those days, one hundred thousand was a very big number. Just to set a frame of reference, my first house in Euclid, Ohio, a three-bedroom brick bungalow, with one-quarter acre of land cost me only forty-nine thousand dollars.

The district manager of Radio Shack was thrilled that I had managed to rack up one hundred thousand dollars in sales working part-time. Most sales persons could not sell as much while working full-time.

One day, he asked me to explain how I had achieved my success to all the sales personnel present at the monthly all-hands district meeting.

I told the sales personnel the following story about how I began selling computer systems and about how the amount of computer sales I had was the primary factor that contributed to my being able to sell over one hundred thousand dollars of merchandise.

In those days, computers were a novelty item, and they cost a minimum of three thousand dollars, and up. Another drawback was that at the time-period in question, Radio Shack was best known for selling pieces and parts not high-end big-ticket items.

What I mean is that most people that came into the store came in with the intention of buying pocket radios, batteries, antennas, alarm clock, speaker wire, etc.

I got started down the path of selling computers quite by accident. I did have one advantage over other Radio Shack sales personnel when it came to computers. I was going to school for my masters in electrical engineering.

Now, do not get me wrong. When I say advantage, I do not mean that I knew how to design computers or repair computers or anything of that sort.

My only advantage was that I had used computers at the University. We had to write book reports and term papers on the green screen VT100 mainframe. Consequently, I was not afraid of computers. That was my only advantage.

Other than that, I knew as much about computers as any other sales person. Moreover, Radio Shack sold the Tandy Color Computers and

IBM PCs. This technology was a far cry from the mainframe technology prevalent in universities at the time.

When I first started working as a sales person at Radio Shack, I read all the mandatory brochures on the different lines of merchandise that we carried. This included car audio, home audio, computers, pieces and parts, etc. I also took and passed some basic proficiency tests on my knowledge of these items.

Computers fascinated me. Whenever the store was slow, I started playing with the three computers that were on display. The store manager advised me not to waste my time on the computers.

He informed me that in order to make commission, I had to average selling fifty-six dollars per hour. Please do not hold me to that exact number. Although, I believe it was fifty-six, it may have been anywhere from fifty-one to fifty-nine.

If I did not exceed the set sales threshold for the week, I only made minimum wage. The store manager also suggested that I try to sell batteries to every customer that came in the store. Actually, his words to the best of my recollection were something like:

"Try pushing batteries to every customer. Everybody needs batteries and you will bump up your sales average."

For a while, I did half-heartedly suggest batteries to every customer that I helped. I needed the job and the store manager was ever watchful.

It was a slow Thursday day in March when I got my break. All I remember is that it was late in the evening and business was very slow.

We had only one customer walk into the store during the previous hour. The manager had already sent all the full timers home. He did not want to hurt their sales averages by making them work slow hours. I was part-time and thereby expendable.

The manager and I were the only two persons left to close the store that day. Closing time was 9:00 PM. Then around 7:45 PM, an older gentleman came into the store and went straight for the surge protector power strips.

There was nothing spectacular about him just an average everyday Joe Customer in casual slacks and a T-shirt. He browsed the power strips, picked one up and began to walk towards to checkout register.

While on his way to the checkout register, he stopped by the computers. I walked over to him, introduced myself and asked him if I could turn one of the computers on for him. He said sure. Then he proceeded to inform me that he had just purchased a computer at the Computer Store.

He also said, "I had no idea that you guys at Radio Shack carried computers."

I began to tell him what I could remember from the brochures about how Tandy was Radio Shack's parent company and how we only sold Tandy approved products. I also told him about the hoard of technicians that we had down in Ft. Worth, TX and how he could bring his computer into any

Radio Shack store should he need it upgraded or fixed down the road.

He asked me many questions about computers in general and about the computers on display in particular. I answered all the questions that I could to the best of my ability. When I did not know the answer to any question, I jotted the question down on a piece of paper and told him that I would find out the answer and have it ready for him the next time he came in.

I did not realize how much time had gone by until I heard the store manager shuffling about and clearing his throat. It was about 8:55 PM and the manager was in the process of shutting down. The discreet (indiscreet) cough was his signal to me to ring out the customer so he could close the drawer for the day.

The entire time, I conversed with this person I addressed him as 'Sir'. I escorted him to the register and rang up his sale for twenty-one dollars and change. As he left, he said; "I am Tom Duffy, you have been very helpful Atul, I will come by next week, if you think you may have the answers to those questions by then."

"I will definitely have the answers for you. I work on Mondays, Wednesdays and Thursday from 4 PM to close." I replied.

"Thank you again for the wonderful conversation, Sir."

When Mr. Duffy left, the store manager glowered at me. He said, "You just let the guy waste over an hour of your time and you did not even sell him batteries."

I distinctly remember his words that day.

He continued; "Remember young man, these people will come in because they have nothing better to do and chat you up just because you are here."

"Never let them leave without selling them something extra."

"That is what makes you a good sales person."

I was thoroughly dejected that day. When I went home, it took me a long while to fall asleep. The words of the sales manager had hurt my feelings. I knew that my sales numbers were not that great during my first month at Radio Shack. Now, I felt like a failure. I was ready to quit.

Then I remembered that I had given Mr. Duffy my word that I would find the answers to his questions that I could not answer earlier. I always keep my word.

I was already bad at sales. I did not want to start down the path of going back on my word in addition. Therefore, I decided to get the answers to those questions, and work another week. I hoped that Mr. Duffy would show up and I could give him the answers and then quit. If he did not show up, I planned work through the week and leave the answers an envelope addressed to Mr. Duffy and quit.

Either way, I had made up my mind not to work as a sales person beyond the next week.

As I mentioned earlier, I was studying electrical engineering. When I went in to school on Friday, I headed straight for the Computer Science (CS) department. I knew several people in the CS department very well.

I located one of them and asked him how I could get answers for the questions on my list. He looked at the range of questions and was perplexed. When I told him that I was trying to help someone out, he suggested a book. I think it was called 'Microcomputer Theory',

I went down to the library, signed the book out and attended classes for the rest of the day. I spent most of Saturday and Sunday reading this book. It was both tedious and fascinating at the same time. Do not ask me how that is possible! I know that sounds like a contradiction in terms.

However, that's exactly what it was. I was fascinated by the things that computers could do and about how they worked. At the same time, I was reading some very boring stuff about BITS and BYTES.

By Sunday evening, I was reasonably knowledgeable about computers. I was definitely not an expert by any stretch of the imagination. I just knew a little bit more than most people.

I went to the university early on Monday, typed out the answers neatly on a word processing machine. I am not sure how many readers are familiar with a word processing machine. It looked a lot like a computer with a keyboard and screen.

However, that is where the similarity ended.

Functionally, all it did was give you the ability to type up a page at a time, read it on the screen and then hit print. Then you cleared the screen and repeated the process for the next page. You could not save anything and if the power went out before you hit print, you lost all your work.

On Monday, I could hardly wait to get through my classes and go into work at 4 PM. Please note that I did not intend to sell anything to Mr. Duffy. After all, he had already informed me that he had just purchased a computer. I was excited because I had the answers to his questions as promised and at the genuine opportunity to help someone.

Well, Monday proved to be an unequivocal disaster and just served to strengthen my resolve to quit at the end of the week. First of all, Mr. Duffy did not put up an appearance. Secondly, the store Manager had told all the fulltime sales persons about how I had wasted one hour of my time for a sale of twenty-one dollars.

All the full timers had something sarcastic and/or condescending to say about my perceived folly. All that evening, I heard comments like,

"Maybe we should change our sign to the free computer counseling clinic"

"With that much time, I could have at least sold him an audio system or a VCR for a couple hundred dollars"

There was only one fulltime salesperson that did not crack jokes at my expense. I do not know where he is now. I still remember his name.

It was Charles Hundley and here is what he said.

"Atul some good will come of this, the universe will never let all that effort you put in go to waste."

"May be you will become a good computer engineer."

"Just ignore the other guys, you are the rookie so they crack jokes at your expense."

"They have all been where you are now."

Here is something else that I find very ironic. A few years ago, I heard Radio Shack's new commercial (slogan). I went something like, "If you've got questions, we've got answers."

My next workday was Wednesday and I really did not want to go into work. All through the day, I thought that I would just call in and quit. When 4:00 PM rolled around, I found myself at the store. I steeled my resolve to work the next two days just as I had decided.

Nothing eventful happened until about 5:30 PM. Not that I expected anything to happen at this stage. In my mind, I had already given up on Mr. Duffy and on this job.

I had resigned myself to the fact that the store manager was correct and I had just wasted my time with Mr. Duffy.

Then at about 5:35PM, in came Mr. Duffy, followed by a younger version of himself and a woman holding on to the arm of the younger person. This time Mr. Duffy was dressed in what looked like a very expensive suit.

He walked straight towards me, stuck out his hand, and said; "How are you today, Atul? This is my son Ed and my daughter-in-law Sylvia."

I exchanged greetings and shook hands with all of them. Then Mr. Duffy said; "Ed and Sylvia work with me. Someday, Ed will take over my practice."

Like an idiot, I repeated; "Practice?"

By the way, let me take this moment to say that I will use some words, language and expressions to explain various incidents as they happened. I am not normally in the habit of using strong (foul) language. However, some incidents will loose their flavor if I try to censor them. Therefore, I apologize in advance if I offend anyone's sensibilities. That is not my intent.

Mr. Duffy replied, "Did I not tell you that I own the Advanced Family Practice in Cleveland?" He handed me his business card. It read Dr. Thomas Duffy followed by a bunch of acronyms and gave the name and address for Advanced Family Medical Practice.

"I apologize if I missed that Dr. Duffy." I replied. "By the way, I have the answers to your questions."

Dr. Duffy turned to his son and said, "What did I tell you Ed, am I not a good judge of character?"

Then he turned to me and said, "I was telling Ed and Sylvia this weekend that I had met a genuinely helpful man."

"I do not think they quite believed me." He continued.

23

"By the way, does Radio Shack have a system for corporate accounts?" he asked.

"Let me check with the store manager Dr. Duffy. Please excuse me for a minute." I replied.

"Before you go Atul, you need to call me Tom, especially if we are going to be doing business."

These words took me completely by surprise. After all, he had already purchased a computer.

I walked over to the store manager in a daze. He had over heard the conversation, he already had a corporate account credit form in his hand and he walked over with me to Dr. Duffy and explained the structure of the form to him.

Dr. Duffy took the form, and said, "We have decided that we need to buy three computers for our practice."

"I do not know exactly what we need. However, here is a list of all the things they should be capable of doing."

He handed me a hand written list in the most atrocious handwriting I have ever seen. I know that medical doctors are supposed to have bad handwriting. However, Dr. Duffy's handwriting more resembled Egyptian hieroglyphs rather than anything in the English language.

He then turned to the store manager and said, "I want to make sure that Atul gets the credit for this sale."

Then, turning back to me he said, "Atul, I will be back on Saturday. Do you think that you can figure out which of your computers will do the stuff I need by then?"

"Definitely Sir" I replied.

"Tom" he said, "remember to call me Tom"

"Yes Tom." I quipped.

"By the way, do you work on Saturday?" He queried.

"I do not work on Saturdays, but, no worries, I will be here." I replied.

"In that case, do not get here before noon. I will come by around noon. We can grab lunch. And call me if you cannot read my scribble."

He said this, and shook my hand. I shook hands with his son and his daughter-in-law and thanked them all.

After they had left, the store manager turned to me and said. "You are one lucky son of a bitch."

"You will probably make bigger numbers in this one sale than most people make selling all month."

I will not tell how much of an effort it was to fight the temptation to say something sarcastic like, "Gee! I guess I really wasted that one hour last Thursday. Did I not?"

Well let us just say that I successfully resisted the temptation to gloat.

Over the next day, I spent several hours on the phone with Tandy Technical Support. I was querying them on how what computer would do all the things Dr. Duffy needed. OH! I skipped classes that day of course.

I learned several things. Dr. Duffy had placed a

tall order. What he needed done could not be done by a standard computer. First, we needed high-end computers. Then we needed some external drives, dot-matrix printers etc. I have never set eyes on most of this stuff except in the Radio Shack master catalog.

I dialed Dr. Duffy's phone number around 4PM on Thursday with considerable trepidation. A woman answered, "Advanced Family Practice, how may I help you."

"May I speak with Dr. Duffy please?" I said.

"Which one Sir?" was the dry response at the other end of the phone?

"Dr. Thomas Duffy please." I replied.

"He is busy at the moment. I can take a message and have him or his nurse call you back." She said.

"Please tell him that Atul from Radio Shack called. I have some……."

She cut me short with the words. "Are you the computer person from Radio Shack?"

"That would be me." I said.

"Please hold." She said. "Let me tell him you are on the line."

A few minutes later Dr. Duffy came on the phone.

"Hello Atul. Having trouble with my handwriting?"

"No Sir, I mean Tom." I said.

"I have figured out what you need, it is a lot of extra equipment."

"I thought as much." He said. "Just make sure

that I am not being taken for a ride."

"I am trusting you on this. We are still on for Saturday right?"

"I will be there at noon." I said.

"Great, I will see you then." And, he hung up.

I went to the store manager and gave him the list of equipment. He looked at the list and asked, "Is he really going to buy all this shit?"

"I just got off the phone with him. He gave the go ahead." I said.

"I just have to re-check this with my computer buddies at school. But I think the list is accurate."

For the first time since I had been working there, he begrudged me some respect. He actually took me into the back room, sat me down, and explained the different sections on a corporate account form to me and showed me how to call it in to Tandy credit. He also taught me how to write up a corporate order.

Then he showed me how to call Tandy fulfillment and check the inventory for other stores in the region. We had to do this because we did not have most of the stuff on Dr. Duffy's list in our store.

I found all the items on the list. Then with the help of the store manager, I filled out store inventory transfer forms. I spent most of Friday evening and Saturday morning driving to several stores collecting this equipment.

It took a little longer than I had planned. Because as soon as I had about three thousand dollars worth of equipment in my car, I drove straight back to my store and unloaded. I did not want to be driving around Cleveland's suburbs with thousands of dollars of equipment in the back seat of my beat-up old Chevy Cavalier.

Dr. Duffy showed up a little after noon. He had already filled out the corporate account credit form. He handed it to me. I called the Tandy Credit Center while he waited. It did not take me long to get approval for a credit line of twenty-five thousand dollars. Apparently, Dr. Duffy had near perfect credit and a lot of money I think.

Incidentally, the total sale came to just over sixteen thousand dollars. After he signed the papers, I loaded all the boxes into his Mercedes.

I knew he had said lunch, but I was unsure about how this was going to work. I did not have to say anything. He said it for me.

"Ed is waiting for us at the practice. Let's dump this stuff, grab him and get lunch. Hop in."

This was my first ride in a Mercedes. It left an impression. I definitely wanted a Mercedes at the time. I have yet to buy my Mercedes. I got interested in SUVs and do not like driving cars any more. I prefer large American-made SUVs. However, that is a long story and I do not want to digress. I do enough of that already.

Ed and I off-loaded the computer equipment into their office building under Tom's watchful eye. Then we went to one of those fancy steak houses. It was the kind of restaurant where every one was dressed down. However, the steaks are thirty dollars apiece. Once again, in the early eighties, thirty dollars was a lot of money for a meal for one person.

While we were eating, Dr. Duffy asked me. "Atul, do you know how all this junk connects together."

"Yes Tom, I even wrote down some additional information that the Technical Support Folks gave me." I said.

"And here is the one-eight-hundred number, just in case you get stuck."

"I don't have the time. Moreover, Ed is a klutz with anything mechanical." Tom Replied.

"I love my son and he is a great physician. However, I would not even let him adjust my alarm-clock radio." He continued.

"No problem Tom, I will help you." I said.

I did not have anything planned. Not knowing how long the corporate account credit forms process would take, I had already planned to work all day Saturday anyway.

Moreover, I could not refuse to help Dr. Duffy after such a sumptuous meal. In addition, I wanted to see how these computers worked. These were the high-end systems not the low-end ones that I played with in the store. Let's just say I was fascinated by them.

I went back with him to their practice. It took me a little over five hours to put the computers together. I turned them on and verified that they worked. I then verified every item on the checklist provided by Tandy Technical Support and showed Tom and Ed how to run their computers.

I was almost finished with setting up the third computer when, Sylvia, Dr. Duffy's daughter-in-law showed up with a large pizza and sodas.

We ate the pizza, and then I showed Sylvia how to run her computer. By the time I was done, it was almost 6:30 PM.

Ed and Sylvia thanked me and left. Dr. Duffy then turned to me and handed me a check for four hundred and eighty dollars. The comments line said, "Computer Consulting Fees."

"Tom" I said, "I cannot accept this."

"Why?" He said. "Did you just win the lottery or something?"

I nodded in the negative.

"Son, listen to me." He continued. "You are still young. You are honest and helpful. I know that you did not come here to help me expecting anything."

"Let me give you some advice Atul." He continued. "Never refuse payment for any services that you perform."

"There is nothing wrong with being compensated fairly for honest work. Always remember that."

I said, "I do not know if store policy permits me to accept anything…"

"Stop right there." He said. "Radio Shack has hired you to be a sales person. Radio Shack did not hire you to be a computer installer."

"Besides you are not on the clock today, am I

correct?" He asked.

"Yes you are Tom." I replied. "Thank you very much."

"Great. Use this to pay you tuition, or buy books or something." He said.

"Let me drive you back to your car."

Dr. Duffy drove me back to the store. It was almost 7:00 PM.

On the way there he said, "By the way, it has to be under five hundred or my accountant will have to give you a 1099 and you will end up paying taxes."

When I walked into the store, the store manager looked at me quizzically and said, "I thought you had been abducted by aliens or something."

I told him about what I had done for Dr. Duffy and showed him the check. He said he did not see any problem with my accepting it.

The only additional thing he said was, "just do not show me those in the future, it makes me jealous."

Then he added, "You made my month kid. I would like to buy you a beer someday."

Apparently, the sale had pushed the store's monthly numbers to a point where the manager made a sizeable bonus. I do not know how much. Moreover, I never got a chance to collect on that beer.

About three weeks after that incident, I went into work one day and the store manager told me that he had instructions to transfer me to another store. He told me to report to the store in Euclid

Mall and ask for the store manager there, a Mr. Paul Circo.

I was filled with anticipation and anxiety. The Euclid Mall store was a legend in the district. It was the only store in the Ohio district that grossed over million dollars in sales every year. It was also one of two stores in the region-5 with the same distinction. I am reasonably certain that region-5 included Ohio, Michigan, Pennsylvania and West Virginia.

Anyway, I guess that detail is not relevant to our discussion. What is relevant is that you had to be among the top sales persons in the district get to work at that store. I had also heard rumors that Paul Circo was being groomed to be the next district manager.

I drove there and asked for Paul Circo. I remember him, for several reasons. One, 'Circo' is an unusual name. Two, he taught me several important lessons that I remember to this day. Over the years, I have lost contact with Paul and do not know his whereabouts. Maybe he will see this book and contact me, if he remembers me.

Anyway, Paul greeted me, and explained why he had asked for my transfer. He said that he realized computers were the next big thing in retail electronics and that he needed someone who understood computers.

He also said that my transfer was not final. I had the right to refuse the transfer. I started to say that I was thankful, and happy, etc.

To which he replied, "Do not thank me yet.

Listen carefully to what I am proposing before you accept."

Paul then proceeded to tell me how he ran his store. He had several sales people that specialized in certain high-ticket items.

He said, "I will not dictate what hours you work on weekdays, as long as you do not exceed sixteen hours."

Paul continued with, "However, you have to work twenty hours on the weekend as follows."

"You will work four hours every Friday evening, and eight hours every Saturday and eight hours Sunday."

Also, you will absolutely be here between the hours of twelve noon and six PM every Saturday and Sunday and work all holidays when I ask you." "These are your only assigned hours. Any additional hours you work are on your own dime."

"Wait there is more." He said. "I do not want you here to sell pieces and parts. I have several minimum wage earners doing that."

He went on to explain that he had several fulltime sales persons who operated the registers and rang up sales for the many customers that walked through the store. He also had another category of sales personnel that specialized in high-ticket items. He had an individual for car audio, an individual for home theater, an individual for scanners and I would be the computer individual.

The way it worked was that we stayed in the part of the store that had our items of expertise and whenever anyone showed interest in our items, regardless of whether we thought they were casual browsers or serious buyers, we gave them the full court press.

If the customer asked about something that was not in our area of expertise, we walked them over to the assigned expert individual made polite introductions and then went back to our area.

This idea sounded very appealing to me. It was not just because I could potentially make high commissions, but also because I was now considered the elite computer person within the district.

The added burden of this newfound fame/notoriety meant that I had to keep reading and studying more about computers. I was also tasked from time-to-time with delivering training sessions to various groups of sales personnel at district meetings.

One of the first things I did after the transfer was to send a card to Dr. Duffy telling him that I was at a different store.

Sure enough, it did not take long for him to come calling. He proved to be my biggest ally and best referral sales generator.

Over the course of the year, Dr. Duffy bought two more computers from me. He also had me install these at his office in my free time and called on me occasionally to teach him things about all the computers that he had bought from me.

Dr. Duffy's accountant ended up sending me the 1099. However, Dr. Duffy also asked his accountant to do my taxes for me that year. The accountant showed me how to offset the income with reimbursement for mileage, business expenses, etc.

Dr. Duffy also referred several of his doctor friends to me. Most of them came to me for advice and ended up buying computers from me. I wish I could say that all my experiences were good. They were not. I guess we do not live in a utopian world after all.

There was this one person in particular who came by with questions all the time. Moreover, the questions became more and more technical over a few weeks. I finally asked him if he was talking about a Tandy computer. He came clean and admitted that he had bought a computer at the computer store. However, no one there was willing to support him after the sale so he kept coming to me to find out information about something he had bought elsewhere.

I asked him for the model number and told him that I would do what I could to help him. However, I did not see him after that day. I guess that he was embarrassed.

The point I am trying to make is that when you achieve a trusted advisor relationship with anyone, do not compromise it just because they are not a near term prospect. They will eventually realize your worth, or maybe they will just feel guilty and buy from you.

Do not take the statement to imply that everyone will buy from you. As I said before, we do not live in a Utopian world. There are people out there who will just use you. In such cases, figure out a diplomatic way to ration your time. Once again, I stress. Do not burn bridges. Just give them less of your time and still provide them advice. Always make certain that your advice is of the highest quality.

The district manager assured me, that having a hundred thousand in sales put me in front of the queue for the next store manager opening. He also assured me that I had a great career ahead of me in Radio Shack. I never found out. About six months later, I graduated and went on to start a short career in information technology consulting followed by a very long career in management consulting, and here I am.

When I tell people this almost three quarters of them ask me if I wonder what would have happened if I had stayed on with Radio Shack. Honestly, I do not know and I do not wonder. I never look at the past. Once I make a decision and take a path, my course is set. I do not second guess myself. If it proves to be a good decision, I revel in my success. If it turns out to be a bad decision, I take my licks, learn my lessons, make certain that I remember the lessons and I move on.

Looking at the past and living in the past only makes us more likely to miss opportunities in the present. I do not remember who told me this but they said, "Shouldda, wouldda, couldda only leads to more Shouldda, wouldda, couldda." They are correct. I say accept, acknowledge, learn and move on.

Oh! My! My! How I have digressed. This chapter was supposed to be about the different types of sales relationships instead it turned out to be pages and pages of words on how I got started in the relationship-selling mode. Without consciously realizing or intending it, I had become the trusted advisor to Dr. Duffy and his friends.

I guess I will write about the different types of relationships that a sales professional can have with clients in the next chapter.

Chapter Three
Types of Relationships - Take 2

As I said before, a sales professional can only have one of two types of relationships with their clients. They are:

- ♦ A Transactional Relationship or
- ♦ A Trusted Advisor Relationship

Some of the statements that I have made in the previous chapter might lead you to think that I believe transactional relationships are bad or inferior. I am not trying to imply that at all. Both types of relationships have their appropriate place in the world of sales.

However, for most corporations and consulting firms, the transactional relationship is not conducive to the longevity and success of the sales professional. For the purposes of this book, I am going to focus on the trusted advisor relationship, as this is the cornerstone of relationship selling.

Once again, I stress that every client-facing individual in a corporation and especially in a consulting organization is a sales professional. Because, their actions and the relationship they establish or do not establish with the client has a bearing on whether your organization will secure the follow-on work on the current project and/or the next opportunity that comes along.

The classic example of a transactional relationship is one that you find in grocery stores, supermarkets etc. You go there to buy a certain commodity, and you do not particularly care who sells it to you as long as they are fast, accurate and courteous.

The classic example of a trusted advisor relationship is a good insurance agent. If they are truly good, you will never buy any type of hazard insurance from another company regardless of the difference in price.

I have that relationship with my insurance agent Steve and his co-agent Joanne. This office has been my agent for everything for more than a decade. They know everything about my life. They insure my life, my house, my vehicles, my yacht, my business, and everything else. Ask me if they are the cheapest in all cases.

The answer is most definitely 'NO.'

However, they are always there when I need them. They understand my needs and my personality. They know most of my quirks. At least the insurance related ones anyway. Believe me, when I say that I have many quirks.

For example, even though I know my blanket policy covers any vehicle I purchase, I will not drive a car from a lot or a yacht out of a marina until I have proof of coverage for the new purchase in my hand.

I know it is silly, but it is a personality quirk, what can I say. I cannot count how many times Joanne has faxed or emailed me paperwork at odd hours just because I asked for something.

A trusted advisor relationship is very hard to attain. It requires a lot of patience and constant effort. It requires absolute unquestionable integrity on your part. Moreover, it can be lost or compromised in the blink of an eye.

A trusted advisor does not try to sell a product; he/she always tries to solve his client's problems. There is never one solution to any problem. The solution is usually a combination of one or all of the following: strategies, processes, technologies and people.

You need to achieve the ability to collaborate with the client and help resolve business problems affecting the organization as a whole.

Easier said than done, you say. You are right. I never said this was easy. In fact, I specifically stated that this would take a lot of patience and constant effort.

I would also like to stress that a trusted advisor relationship is not the same as a "buddy" relationship. Sure, I rely on my friends to provide me with ad hoc advice. In fact we all do. However, would you let your buddy diagnose your health problems or do you go to a trusted source (a qualified doctor). Now think about how you select a new doctor. You very rarely go to the first doctor you stumble across unless it is an emergency or an urgent matter that cannot wait.

You typically ask your friends, neighbors, or relatives for their experiences with various doctors and try to go see the doctor who they recommend. The point I am trying to make is that you use your friends and buddies for advice. However, you rely on the trusted and qualified professional (the doctor) to help resolve your problem.

Therefore, it is most important for the client to perceive you more as the person who they can trust to provide the appropriate solution and less as the person who is their friend or buddy.

The modern sales professional, especially one that wants to follow the doctrine of relationship selling, must move away from the traditional transactional sales solution.

The client should view you and someone who they can rely on to help them succeed no matter what the circumstances. You need to evolve from a person who recommended and sold systems or devices to a person who collaborates with the client and helps resolve business problems affecting the organization as a whole, or a specific problem that affects that client in person.

When you achieve this, you will have morphed in your client's eyes. He/she will no longer view you as a sales person but as a trusted advisor.

Chapter Four
Establishing Trusted Relationships

The key to establishing trusted relationships is genuineness, respect, sincerity and above all honesty.

I am going to use an analogy that is probably going to annoy or offend some readers but it is the only one I can think of at the moment.

Let us assume that you go to the bar strictly looking for a one-night stand. It does not matter whether you are male or female. You have certain criteria of the type of man or woman you are looking to sleep with. When you find that person, you will say and/or do whatever it takes to get them to bed. Because, that is all you want.

Your interest in that person does not go beyond that one night. Therefore, it really does not matter what you say to them. When the morning comes, your interactions with that person are finished. You could tell them that you are King/Queen of England if that is what it takes to get them into bed.

On the contrary, if you are looking for a long-term relationship, hopefully, you do not start out by lying to the person in question. Every psychologist will tell you that healthy long-term relationships are based on respect and trust.

A client relationship is much the same. The transactional relationship is like the one-night stand. Your interest in the client is just for that one transaction. You do not care as long as you close the current transaction.

On the other hand, the trusted advisor relationship is a long-term relationship. It takes a lot of time and effort.

Let us examine the aspects of the trusted relationship.

Genuineness: If you are going to make a career as a trusted advisor and follow the doctrine of relationship selling, you need to be a genuine person. This means that:

- You should be genuinely interested in people.
- You should be genuinely interested in helping others without expectations.
- You should have a genuine desire to make friends.
- You should have a genuine belief in yourself and in the goodness of others. and
- You should have a genuinely positive outlook on life.

If all this sounds like a bunch of malarkey / hooey to you, let me explain. Trusted advisor relationships are long-term relationships. They take a longtime to nurture and require a lot of patience.

You cannot fake any aspect of your client relationship over a long period. Therefore, you need to be genuinely interested in people and interested in helping other people without expectations.

Think back to the Dr. Duffy scenario. If I had not been genuinely interested in helping him, what do you think would have happened when he told me that he had just bought a computer?

- ◆ I may have walked away from him.
- ◆ I may have given him only cursory attention or worse yet,
- ◆ I may have been curt or perhaps even rude with him.

How then would I have achieved the trusted advisor relationship that helped me achieve the accolade of exceeding one hundred thousand dollars in sales that year?

You also need to be genuinely positive. This is a cultivated behavior. I suggest that you consciously cultivate the ability to see the positive in everything. A genuinely positive person is like a breath of fresh air. Most people (Clients are people) do not like to interact with pessimistic people.

Think about what you do when faced with a pessimistic person. I personally limit my interactions with such an individual to that which is absolutely necessary. I am not saying that I am rude or anything. Just that I limit my interactions with pessimistic people.

If your client perceives you as pessimistic, they will potentially limit their interactions with you. Ask yourself if you will succeed in establishing a trusted advisor relationship in that case. I am sure the answer you came up with is 'NO.'

You also need to have a genuine belief in yourself and in the goodness of others. If you do not have faith in others, you will look at everything and everyone with suspicion.

There is a lot more than just saying the right words when establishing a successful trusted advisor relationship. Your body language and what you leave unsaid plays a large role.

Have you ever encountered a person where you feel that something is just not right? Think about it. They say all the right words but something inside you keeps telling you that it just does not sound right. This is because the person does not genuinely believe what they are saying. Would you feel comfortable with such a person being your trusted advisor?

My point exactly! This is why I stress that genuineness is critical to establishing trusted relationships.

Respect: The process of being genuine naturally leads to having the same level of respect, attitude and behavior towards everyone, regardless of whether they are your boss, employee, co-worker, waiter, barber, grocery clerk, etc.

This again is a cultivated habit and not as easy as it sounds. We are programmed from childhood to have a level of deference and respect to people in positions of authority. I am sure you have heard statements that are similar in meaning to the following, if not verbatim.

- ◆ "Do not talk back to your teachers"
- ◆ "Show respect when talking with the principal"
- ◆ "Respect your elders"
- ◆ "Address the police as Sir or Ma'am"

Do you ever recall hearing statements like the following?

- ◆ "Show the same respect to the janitor as the principal"
- ◆ "Treat your employees just like you would treat your boss"
- ◆ "Address the grocery clerk as Sir or Ma'am"
- ◆ "Treat your fellow students just like you would treat a teacher"

I am willing to make a bold statement that not more than twenty percent of you answered yes to that question. It would actually give me great joy if someone proves me wrong on this statistic.

I am trying to instill this behavior in my son Cory (a typical teenager) with some interesting occurrences along the way.

Just last week, we were at the grocery store and I addressed the grocery clerk as "ma'am."

Cory tells me, "Don't call her ma'am, she goes to my high school. She is a senior. Her name is Ashley"

My response was, "Cory, I address all grocery clerks as sir or ma'am, because they address me as sir"

Cory's quick retort was, "What about Roland, you call him by his name." I guess it is time for me to mention that Cory is very intelligent, sometimes too smart for his own good. Nevertheless, he had an excellent point in this case.

Roland is the seafood clerk at the grocery store where we have shopped for the past five or six years. Roland and I had established a relationship based on our mutual interest in fishing, cooking fish and enjoying fish dishes.

My response to Cory was, "Cory how long have we known Roland?"

"About five-years I guess?" Cory answered

"Cory, over those five years I got to know Roland very well and somewhere along the way, Roland and I started calling each other by first names."

"So now, I call him Roland and he calls me Atul."

I said. "'With regards to your friend Ashley, you know her from school, so she calls you Cory and you call her Ashley."

"However, she only knows me, as your Dad and/or the guy who shops for groceries."

"Therefore she calls me sir and I call her ma'am." "Does that make sense?" I asked.

Cory's response was, "I guess"

I hope that I got through to him.

Showing respect for all individuals regardless of their stature in society or an organization will earn you more respect, trust and goodwill than any other trait.

We recently had our driveway re-poured and our patio re-done. The principal contractor came by early on a Saturday morning, delivered instructions to the crew and left.

It was a hot and humid day with daytime temperatures predicted to reach ninety-five degrees. A little after ten, Patricia and I went to the store, bought a twelve pack of bottled water, a twelve pack of Gatorade and some ice.

We put the bottled water and Gatorade in a cooler with the ice and set it in a shady location in our yard. I then informed the person that appeared to be the site-lead that we had beverages for him and his crew in the cooler. We also told him that we would order a couple of pizzas for all of them around noon.

The site-lead was very surprised that we would be so nice to them. Patricia promptly told him that they were guests on our property and we treat all our guests the same. He proceeded to tell us some of his experiences.

I am just going to recount one. The site-lead informed us that on a similarly hot and humid day, he had knocked on the door of the house where they were doing concrete work and requested some water. Apparently, the homeowner had told them that there was a garden hose in the back and that they should drink out of it.

I cannot comprehend the rationale behind this mode of thinking. These people are working on your house/property. You should treat them very nicely, if for no other reason, simply to ensure that they are well motivated while doing a job for you.

The Pizza's, Gatorade, water and ice cost us only about twenty-five dollars. However, let me tell you, the additional work that these people did and the additional care that they took was probably worth ten times more. Most importantly, we generated goodwill. They were very happy to be working at our house. As a result, they did not rush and they did a thorough job.

I have experienced, time and time again, that it is these small, simple, seemingly insignificant things that matter the most. Surveys have found that in a corporate environment, bringing doughnuts for your colleagues or your employees on occasion produces more loyalty and willingness to put in extra work than a pay raise. Think about it!!!

Sincerity and Honesty: How is genuineness different from sincerity and honesty? It is simple really. Genuineness relates to the core of your values. You could be a genuinely nice person. You could also be a genuinely dishonest person.

Sincerity and honesty relate to your ethics, values and your ability to tell the truth regardless of the consequences. Just like genuineness, there is no way to fake sincerity and honesty over the long run.

Your client needs to perceive you as a sincere and honest person in order to trust you. You develop this trust by consistently meeting set expectations.

Trust is the result of consistently fulfilled promises. You can demonstrate sincerity and honesty by practicing and exhibiting the behaviors listed below.

♦ Do not hide negative information from the client.

♦ Do not put a positive or a negative spin on information when presenting it to the client.

♦ Always state the facts and present a balanced picture including both positive and negative information.

♦ Make promises that you can keep.

♦ Go one-step further – under promise and over deliver.

♦ Do not gossip with, to or about the client.

♦ When issues arise, (Trust me they will, there is no one who can honestly state that they have never had unexpected client delivery issues and challenges), meet the client with the attitude of lets work it out.

♦ Do not pass blame to others (especially client personnel).

♦ If you are the one at fault, apologize once, and proceed with a plan to fix the issue.

- ♦ Do not overly dwell on the negative.
- ♦ Maintain a positive can do attitude. AND above all
- ♦ Do not compromise your personal integrity for anyone or anything.

Just like everything in this book, the steps I have identified above seem simple. It is not rocket science. It is just basic values and commonsense. Most of you know everything in here already. The trick is recognizing it and using it consistently.

Sure, it is commonsense. Nevertheless, to quote from one of my other books, "Common sense in an uncommon degree is what the world calls wisdom."

Chapter Five

Etiquette

Etiquette is an often overlooked but very important factor in you ability to establish and maintain successful client relationships. Ignorance of workplace etiquette can and will doom you.

No matter what you do or what position you hold, the way you dress and present yourself can have a major impact on your success. Despite claims to the contrary, people always judge you by the image you project. Competition is fierce and your image can be an asset or a hindrance.

The question "what is etiquette?" always elicits responses like "good manners," "politeness," "respect," etc. The encyclopedia Britannica uses the following statements to define and discuss etiquette.

- ♦ A system of rules and conventions that regulate social and professional behavior in any given environment
- ♦ These are norms of behavior mandated by custom and enforced by group pressure
- ♦ An offender faces no formal trial or sentence for breach of etiquette; the penalty lies in the disapproval from peers and superiors

Proper etiquette dictates that you practice different kinds of behavior at home, at your favorite social hangout, and at work. If you start treating your client, your boss and your coworkers the same way you treat people you hang out with at the corner bar, you are asking for big trouble.

Some general concepts apply to workplace etiquette in all forms, no matter who you are dealing with, and no matter what form your interactions take. The list below states the basic guidelines to managing all business relationships:

- ◆ Respect and Kindness: Every person you work with deserves respectful treatment. Even if you dislike someone, you will come out on top if you maintain a respectful manner.

- ◆ Appearance: Always go to work well groomed and dress appropriately for your position and work place. Most companies have both written and unwritten rules about appropriate attire. Dressing appropriately is especially crucial with the increase of international business. Americans are incredibly casual compared to international businesspersons. People in the international business environment see it as a sign of disrespect.

- ◆ Cultural Awareness and Deference: Leave gender, race, marital status, political preference, sexual preference, etc. out of the equation. Always maintain an appropriate level of deference. Always act with respect and consideration for everyone, regardless of his or her position, age, or status.

♦ Honesty and Integrity: Be honest, ethical and above reproach in all your business dealings.

♦ Language and Slang: Always talk like a professional. Do not use slang, rude, derogatory, or obscene language, no matter whom you are addressing.

♦ Cyber-etiquette: An e-mail is a written document that can be printed and forwarded, so use proper grammar and check the spelling for all office communications. Do not use the office email address to send or receive personal emails.

♦ Respect Personal Space: Everyone has his or her own amount of personal space that acts as an invisible border. Never touch someone other than to shake hands or politely tap a shoulder to get attention.

♦ Observe the Corporate Culture: Every company has rules of behavior even if they are unwritten. If everyone in your office dresses in business attire, do the same. In some workplaces, it is acceptable to walk over and chat with co-workers. In others it is taboo. You can avoid most pitfalls by carefully observing and going with the flow.

KEY INTERPERSONAL SKILLS

- There are some skills that you will always need in business.
- Introductions
- Eye Contact and
- Handshake

These three things seem to confound and terrify many people. When in fact they are very simple, and can easily become second nature with a little practice.

Introducing Yourself And Others

A cliché states something to the effect that you make your first impression within the first thirty seconds of meeting someone new. This is very true and if that impression is bad, you have to work very hard to overcome the setback.

Think about what you typically do in the first thirty seconds of meeting someone. Yes! You introduce yourself (and maybe your colleagues) to the individual to individuals that you are meeting.

Introducing yourself to someone you have not met before is definitely challenging. How do you go about it? Let us look at three scenarios below:

- You go to their office location

- ♦ They come to your office location
- ♦ You meet at a neutral location like a restaurant.

One simple introduction works in all these scenarios. I personally use it almost all the time. "Hi, I am Atul from LMN Corporation. Thank you for taking the time to meet with me (us – if you have a colleague with you)." Then I pause and give them a chance to introduce themselves.

Note:

- ♦ I use only my first name
- ♦ I do not state my title
- ♦ I thank them

These three factors put my counterparts at ease and let them know that their time is important to me and I appreciate their time.

Introducing third party personnel (who have not met prior) to each other can be equally as challenging. Especially since this usually involves introducing a client to your boss or a senior personal in your organization.

Here is how I typically handle the introduction.

"Peter, this is John Smith, our Vice President of Operations, John, this is Peter West. He's the Director of Federal Markets at XYZ Corporation."

In the above example, Peter is the client and John is my colleague.

Note:

- ♦ I always first introduce my colleague to the client
- ♦ Then I introduce the client to my colleague

Remember that eventually, you are going to end up in the embarrassing situation where you forget the name of someone you are just about to introduce.

Here is what I do in this scenario. "I am sorry, my mind just blanked out on your name, Please remind me." Then I proceed with your normal introduction.

Note:

- ♦ Do not try to cover up the fact that you forgot someone's name
- ♦ Apologize once and do not make a big deal of the situation

Eye Contact

Proper eye contact is very critical, especially in business. Good eye contact conveys many subtle messages. It signals, honesty, integrity, openness and demonstrates confidence. If you do not make eye contact during a conversation, you will most likely give the impression that you lack confidence and that you are hiding something. This may lead people to believe that you are shifty and untrustworthy.

Remember, eye contact is not the same as staring. DO NOT stare at people, it makes them uncomfortable. Good eye contact simply means looking someone directly in the eye during a conversation.

Shaking Hands

A proper handshake conveys confidence, acceptance and extends a gesture of welcome. Shaking someone's hand is very simple. Extend your hand crisply, but do not look at their hand. Grasp the hand firmly, shake gently once or twice and let go. Remember the hand shake is not a "who can crush who's hand contest" or "who can pull who's arm out of their shoulder socket contest."

Conversely, do not leave you hand limp or give only your fingers to the other person's grasp.

The biggest error that you can make is refusing to accept a hand someone has extended. Refusing a handshake is perceived as a sign of ill will or rejection.

You cannot go wrong with etiquette if you always try to act like you would if your mom was watching you.

Cell Phone & Blackberry Etiquette (this is my pet peeve)

When you are meeting with a client, there is nothing more important at that moment in time than the client. Let me emphasize. When I say nothing I mean "NOTHING"

My employees are all aware that if I ever catch them or hear of them responding to a cell phone call or typing away at a blackberry while in a meeting with a client or during a formal meeting with their colleagues, I will terminate their services.

There is only one exception that I will accept.

♦ An ongoing family emergency or situation:

I was in this situation at one point in my career. It was the time when Patricia (my wife) was undergoing some serious medical issues. I was away from work for almost a month. However, some unavoidable meetings came about that I could not reschedule, cancel or send a representative in my stead.

When I attended to these meetings, I started my informing the client that I had an ongoing family situation that may require me to answer my cell phone should I get a call from the hospital and it could potentially result in me having to leave the meeting.

Almost all clients will be sympathetic to your situation and actually respect you for informing them upfront. I would then place the phone on vibrate and look at it if it vibrates. Further, I would ignore all other calls except the one that came from the hospital.

There is absolutely no excuse for using a blackberry during a meeting. No email is so important that it cannot wait for an hour. If you tell me that, you have emails that are so important that they cannot wait. I have one comment and one question for you.

- Do not attend meetings. Just stay in your office and answer your emails.
- How did you conduct business prior to the blackberry phenomenon?

I remember attending a board meeting several years ago when blackberries first became available. A Senior Vice President named John was furiously responding to emails on his blackberry. The Chairman of the Board, Stan, Stopped the board meeting and asked the following to John.

"John, has the fire department arrived yet?"

"What fire department?" Was John's surprised reply?

Stan said, "I assumed that since you were emailing something during my meeting that it was something really important, like that your house was on fire or something."

"And if it is not that, I suggest that you turn that device off and give us the courtesy of your attention", Stan continued.

I have recounted this story to several people and they feel that Stan was being rude and cruel to John.

I will concede that Stan was harsh, however, who was really being rude here?

Here is what I read from John's actions: All the people gathered at this meeting are less important than my emails

Now that I have gone on about my pet peeve, let me tell you what I recommend.

- When you attend a meeting (any meeting, not just a client meeting), turn off your cell phone and/or blackberry. At minimum, change it to silent mode.
- Do not look at your phone or blackberry until after the meeting is completed
- Do not under any circumstance respond to emails or answer cell phone calls when with a client unless
- It concerns the business of that particular client AND
- It is relevant to the meeting at hand.
- Never answer your cell phone or blackberry when at lunch or dinner with a client.
- For that matter, never answer you cell phone or blackberry when at lunch or dinner with your family. Think about the message that you are sending to your family when you respond to cell phone calls and/or blackberries at dinner.
- Always take into account how you would feel if you were on the receiving end of someone's lack of cell phone etiquette.
- If you have an ongoing family emergency or situation that may necessitate you having to respond to your cell phone, do the following.
- Inform the client (or senior meeting

attendee) of the situation.

◆ Turn the cell phone to vibrate mode.

◆ Respond only if it is the number that signifies it is the emergency call

◆ Thank the client in advance for their understanding.

I am not going to delve into etiquette in any more detail.

There are several sources available with good information. Information on etiquette is available at the following web sites:

http://www.businessoftouch.com/index2.html
http://www.ravenwerks.com/practices/etiquette.htm
http://www.ryangrpinc.com/etiquette_tips_business.asp

Chapter Six
Groping the Grouper

I am not going to spend a lot of time on this chapter, as this is an example of something not to do. I prefer to focus on the positive. However, I cannot help but mention this incident.

"Groping the Grouper" is the term that is commonly used to describe insincere efforts to establish trusted relationships. This may work some of the time, however it seldom works over any lengthy period. By the way, Grouper is a type of fish.

Here is my personal experience with a Groping the Grouper scenario.

SETUP: An insincere sales professional walks into the office of a prospective client (Atul). Let us call the sales professional 'Jim'.

Jim was trying to get me to buy their accounting software package for my firm. He claimed it was better than what we had and would help us with our government reporting requirements, etc.

Jim understood some of the concepts of relationship selling. However, he did not grasp or did not want to invest the time in following the principles of genuineness, respect, sincerity and honesty. He wanted to use the short cut method.

After the customary exchange of greetings and pleasantries, Jim said, "Bob told me that you caught a huge fish last year."

Incidentally, Bob was my Director or Operations at the time. He had met with Jim in the prior week and had recommended that I meet with Jim.

A very important thing to note here is that Jim is not an angler. (I found this out later, of course.)

I replied, "Yeah I did. It weighed sixty-three pounds. I caught that Tuna about three years ago just off the coast."

"It took me almost an hour to reel him in."

Jim said, "That is great Atul, I love fishing too. My buddies and I are always out there every opportunity we get."

Jim continued, "I usually love to use a buck-tail jig with some strip bait on it."

"I have never had the skill to catch something big like you."

"I mostly get smaller fish two or three pounders"

I never said Jim was unintelligent. He had obviously read articles on fishing. I only said that he was insincere. He had in fact never fished. (Another piece of information that I found later, of course.)

I told Jim, "I usually run a big game trolling lure with an 11/0 or 12/0 hook on my penn-senator rod with a hundred pound test mono-filament line with a braided steel leader"

"I also have a spoon rigged on a light cast rod just in case my wife and I run into a school of blue fish."

Jim really turned the charm on, he said, "Atul, you are really lucky, I wish my wife loved to fish."

"I get out on the water every chance I get, but my wife does not like it."

At the time, I was pleased to meet a fellow angler and empathized with his situation. Therefore, I offered the following.

"Tell you what Jim, my wife and I love having guests on our boat."

"Let me figure out our schedule over the four to six weeks and we can go out on some Friday or Saturday. I will also ask Bob to join us."

A point of note, I may be the captain of my boat. However, my lovely wife is the undisputable chief of operations. Therefore, if I want to invite someone, I check with her to ensure that she has not planned something already.

Coming back to my conversation with Jim, I continued, "In the mean time Jim, schedule a demo with my accounting staff and show them the capabilities of your product."

Over the next month or so, I saw Jim in passing at my office several times. He was conversing with my accounting staff and with Bob.

I think it was about five (maybe six) weeks later that the boat schedule opened up.

Here is another one of my quirks. My wife and I will entertain guests on our boat on a Friday or Saturday. Sunday is always reserved for immediate family time – no exceptions.

I asked Bob what he thought of going out fishing with Jim in tow. Bob and his wife Sandra were guests on our boat at least once or twice every year.

Bob accepted and communicated with Jim. I presume that he also gave Jim directions to the marina.

We went out on a Saturday. Bob & Sandra arrived first at the marina, my wife (Patricia) and I arrived a few minutes after them, and Jim arrived a few minutes after we did.

After Bob & I introduced Jim to our respective wives, we proceeded down the dock to my boat.

My wife always gets on me when I keep saying boat. Before I get into too much trouble with her, I must mention that the boat I refer to is actually an Islander Custom Yacht forty-five feet in length with a beam (width for you land lubbers) of twelve and a half feet. It has a full galley (kitchen), head (toilet) with shower and one stateroom (master suite). It also has the capacity to sleep eight.

The reasons I mention this is that waves of two or three feet are not an issue when you are on this vessel. You are on the water so it is going to roll. However, it is not going to be like going out on a twenty-foot johnboat. The Islander displaces over twenty-two thousand pounds and delivers a very comfortable ride even in rough seas.

Jim seemed very excited about the trip and could not contain his enthusiasm. He kept thanking me for the opportunity to enjoy his favorite pastime.

He oooed and aaahed over the various features of the boat and marveled at its cleanliness. This made Patricia very happy. Patricia is a very gracious host and very meticulous also. She ensures that the boat in immaculate condition at all times and well stocked with food and other necessities.

The weather forecast for the day was ten to twelve knot winds with swells of one or two feet. We set sail at about 8:00 AM.

Patricia and I have a routine when we go out on the water. I rig and check all rods that we plan to use prior to leaving the dock. As soon as I am clear of the marina and in the channel, she gets the rods on deck and sets them up.

It usually takes us about an hour to get to the area where we like to fish.

The Saturday in question was no different. Once we got to where we wanted, I slowed down to about four knots (trolling speed) and Patricia cast the trolling baits and lures into the water making sure that they were running about fifty-feet behind the boat.

Once the rods were set, Patricia brought up cheese and crackers, fruit, soft drinks, water, etc. for us to snack. Here is where the fun began. Bob, Sandra, Patricia and I start munching on snacks and waiting for something to happen with the rods. Jim did not seem quite at ease. He refused to eat or drink anything.

Finally, Patricia asks him if he is feeling unwell. His response was that he might have a touch of acid reflux. We always have a full medical kit on board in case of emergencies. So Patricia, (the always-dutiful host that she is), went below deck to bring up some antacids.

Jim chewed on the antacids and seemed to feel better.

After a few minutes, Jim piped up, "So Atul, what do you think of the accounting package."

Now it was Bob's turn to lose color in his face. Bob knows the cardinal rule on the boat. No business discussions period!

In addition, I am certain that Bob informed Jim about this rule.

My response was, "Jim, I am sure Bob told you that we do not discuss business on the boat."

"We are here to relax and enjoy a day on the water." I continued.

This is where Jim made his second mistake by saying, "Absolutely Atul, I respect that and I am not trying to discuss business.

"I just want to know what you think of the package."

I am a reasonably patient man and I do not lose my cool very often. However, I will not be pushed beyond a certain point.

Bob could see that Jim was getting very close to pushing me beyond that point.

Therefore, he jumped in with the following, "Jim, the team has not yet briefed Atul on the demo and what we learned about your product."

Just about that time, one of the lines started to sing. Patricia and I almost simultaneously said "Fish on."

Patricia continued, "Jim you are the first-time guest, how about you get this one."

Meanwhile, I got the rod out of the rod holder and handed it to Jim. Jim grabbed the rod from me and started cranking to like a man possessed.

I stopped him and said, "Jim, Jim, hold on there for a second, you did not set the lever."

I set the lever so that Jim was actually reeling in the line and not just cranking the handle.

As soon as I did this, Jim, felt the strain of the fish on the line. He kept on trying to fight it. Therefore, Bob and I started with fishing 101.

"Jim, lean back and pull the rod up using your legs and back."

"Then as you lean forward drop the rod and reel in the line"

"Then lean back again and repeat the process."

Jim fought this fish as if his very existence depended on it. He was perspiring profusely, straining himself, and fighting with the rod instead of letting the rod work for him.

He interspersed his strenuous activities with comments like

"It feels like there is at least fifty pounds out there." And,

"Boy this is going to be one big sucker."

When he finally pulled it in, it turned out to be a bluefish that probably weighed about five pounds. Then he tried to reach for the hook with his bare hands.

Patricia and I both jumped up to stop him.

I said, "Careful Jim. A blue fish will take your finger off if you put your hand near his mouth."

I will not bore you with the details but gradually over the course of the next few hours, it became apparent to us that Jim had almost no experience with boating and even lesser experience with fishing.

The incident that I would categorize as the proverbial last straw occurred at about two in the afternoon. The wind direction changed just a little and we were in about three feet swells.

Without warning Jim rushed to the side, leaned over the gunwale (pronounced gunnel), and puked his guts out.

He recovered himself paused a minute or so and then leaned over again. Except this time, he leaned out too far and this time he fell overboard.

Patricia and I rushed into our well-practiced man overboard drill. She threw him a ring buoy while I turned the boat around and brought it alongside Jim. Then Bob and I grabbed Jim and hauled him back onboard.

Patricia rushed down below deck and brought up some dry towels for Jim. After he dried himself off, I loaned him my extra pair of sweats that I always keep onboard.

Patricia knew exactly what I was thinking. It is amazing how that woman can read my mind. While Jim was down below changing, she came to my side and whispered, "Honey, let it go, just don't say anything."

However, I could not just leave it be. When Jim came back up, I asked him, "Jim have you ever been on a boat before?"

Jim stuttered and stalled for a moment and then says, "Well actually Atul, I have not."

I said, "I guess you have never fished before either?"

Jim said, "I did go fishing once with my grandfather when I was a kid."

I said, "Jim it appears that you lied to me just to sell me your software package."

"I just wanted to make you trust me," was Jim's infuriating response.

I said, "Jim, I do not want to belittle you."

"However, I must point out to you that you do not make someone trust you by lying to them."

"You earn their trust by your actions and with the truth."

That pretty much ruined the trip and I turned the boat back. No one said much on the return journey. When we got back to the dock, Jim thanked Patricia and I and took his leave.

Bob, Sandra, Patricia and I hung-out on the boat for a few hours and we went to the Surf-Side restaurant for dinner.

Most of our conversation was trivial. However, there was one thing Bob said that stuck in my mind.

Bob said, "I wish Jim hadn't pulled this crap on us. The accounting team really liked the package."

"I guess you are not going to buy from him are you?"

Bob was correct. I did not buy from Jim. Jim tried calling one or twice and apologized. However, I firmly informed him that I did not intend to buy from him.

If Jim had not pulled a "Groping the Grouper" trick on me, and he had just established a genuine trusted relationship even if it was based solely on work related items, I most probably would have bought the software based purely on the fact that my accounting team liked the functionality.

My company does a lot of Federal business and our current package was not capable of fulfilling some new reporting requirements. Therefore, we needed to upgrade our accounting software.

We eventually bought a competing accounting software package, and Jim lost a sale because of his dishonesty.

In closing this chapter, I stress again that this is a classic example of what not to do. Genuineness, respect, sincerity and honesty are the cornerstones to trusted relationships.

Chapter Seven
The Lust Technique

What does LUST have to do with relationship selling or with being a trusted advisor? LUST has everything to do with your relationship with your client. LUST is a technique that will get you out of jams.

It is designed to always keep you in the trusted advisor mode and keep you from falling in to the transactional sales mode as long as you use it consistently.

The following four skills define the LUST technique:

- Listening
- Understanding
- Soliciting Input
- Trusted Advice

If you are wondering how these four skills will help you establish and maintain a trusted relationship with your client or get you out of difficult situations, let me tell you.

Listening is a key skill. Just observe carefully and note the exact moment when you start thinking about what you are going to say in any conversation. You will realize that most times, you hear just enough to get the gist of what the other person is trying to say in the conversation and then begin thinking about your response. Have you really listened to them?

The answer is no.

True listening goes way beyond just hearing the words of the person speaking to you. It involves listening to what they leave unsaid. It also means observing their body language and giving them your complete undivided attention.

I have repeatedly encountered circumstances where people start thinking about what they are going to say after hearing long enough to gather the gist of the message. In doing so, they miss the entire hidden meaning of the message. All they manage to gather is what was conveyed by the words.

For example a client who tells you, "If you do not complete the project on time, I will terminate your contract and sue you," might actually be conveying the following.

"I am afraid my bosses will fire me if this does not work."

In addition, "I will try to make you my scapegoat before I go down." OR

"If I go down for this I am taking you with me."

If your listen to the unsaid message and show understanding and empathy for it, you will make this client your ally. You will realize that you both have a stake in making this work.

Understanding and empathy is your way of showing the client that you have actually listened to their stated and unstated message. Please note that I am not asking you to blurt out the unsaid message to the client just because you get it.

Respond to the client in their language. Be as subtle or as open as they are. Please use your best judgment.

In the example above, I would not respond to the client by saying, "I guess you will be fired if this project does not work?"

How about mentioning something like, "Mr. Client, I realize how critical it is for you and your management to get this project working on time and within budget."

By mentioning his management, what you have effectively said without saying the actual words is, "Mr. Client, I understand that you are getting a lot of heat from your management."

Usually when you convey your understanding to the client, they are ready to accept you and listen to your ideas. However, I caution you not to make the mistake of giving them ideas at this stage.

You might be tempted. You might think you know exactly what the client needs. You may even be correct in your assumption that you know exactly what the client needs. However, anything you say at this time will be your opinion and yours alone. You have not made the client part of the decision process by soliciting their input.

Soliciting the client's input serves two critical purposes. First and most importantly, it makes the client part of the process. This is the most critical step towards client buy in. Anything that you develop after soliciting the clients input becomes part of a joint ownership.

The fact that they are your ideas and that you thought of them way before soliciting the client's input has no bearing at this time. Anyway, this is exactly how you want it to be.

If you have your client's buy in to the process, you can rest assured that they will support your solution. They will also help you achieve the results and defend (justify) the solution to their organization. Because inside they believe that, they have ownership in the decision. It is in fact their baby.

Once you have achieved the client's buy in, you are ready to deliver trusted advice. Let us further examine what we mean by the words "Trusted advice."

Providing Trusted Advice is the process of furnishing your client with objective information that is beneficial for the client. The catch is that you have to do this in a way that it makes the client feel that they are part of the decision making process. The client cannot feel, lectured, chastised, forced, or cornered into the decision.

Let me give you an example of something that happened just last week. My team is on a special consulting assignment for a government agency that has some OMB compliance issues.

My team had created a PowerPoint presentation for the client to deliver to the OMB. One of the slides had some mention of the Federal Enterprise Architecture. When we presented the draft to the client, the client (let us call her Maureen) did not like one of the graphics.

Her response was, "I want a red circle around this box." One of my consultants, obviously the one that had created the graphic immediately piped up and said, "Does it have to be red?"

Maureen said, "Yes, I want a red circle, right here." She proceeded to draw a circle with her finger around the box in question.

At this point, I interjected and said, "OK Maureen, noted, will do."

I could see that my smart, young (inexperienced) employee was getting ready to start a discussion with the client about why he did not think we needed a red circle, and I wanted to avoid that at all costs.

After the meeting, I asked my employee what his objections were to the red circle. He explained to me that a red circle in that place would throw the taxonomy of the entire presentation astray. Apparently, they were already using red circles to denote items on the critical path etc. His point was valid.

I asked him what he would recommend to accommodate the client. He suggested that we change the outline of the box to blue and the fill color to yellow. That way it would still stand out and not interfere with the taxonomy.

Therefore, I went back to Maureen (the Client) and told her, "Maureen, my team is making the changes as discussed."

"In the mean time, I wanted to go over the taxonomy of the presentation, so that you are ready just in case someone at OMB asks you questions."

We went over the taxonomy of all the various symbols and objects. I then suggested that we go through all the slides and review them so she was clear.

When we came to the slide in question, the one where she insisted on having the red circle, I paused for a second as if studying the slide and said, "We are putting a red circle here…." Then I paused again for half a second.

I did not have to do anything more, Maureen did the rest.

She said, "That would make the Federal Enterprise Architecture box look like it is on the critical path."

"We cannot have that."

I interjected with, "What did you want to depict with that box?"

She said, "I want to make sure that it stands out from the rest."

I replied, "How about, I have the team change the outline to a different color say blue and fill the box yellow."

"That will make it stand out."

"What do you think?"

"That is a great idea." She replied.

I had given advice to a client without lecturing, forcing, chastising etc.

The LUST technique in action:

Let me tell about you another real life experience where this technique helped me save a critical client relationship. It also resulted in getting a payment of almost seven million dollars that the client was refusing to pay. It also helped me avoid a lawsuit and secure follow-on work to the tune of eight million dollars.

All this happened at one client site over a span of two weeks. I may not have even got past the first day were it not for this technique.

In addition, when the incident started, I had no relationship with this client – far cry from a trusted relationship. Prior to the day in question, I had only spoken to the client once over the phone and never met the client face-to-face.

In 1996, some of my venture capitalist friends, asked me to join a company in which they had invested heavily. They were convinced that the company had the potential for acquisition by a larger firm. However, client satisfaction issues and delivery issues plagued the company.

They asked me to join the company as the Vice President of Professional Services (a sort of board stooge, I guess). They wanted me to fix the delivery issues at this company and get it ready for sale.

They gave me nine months to accomplish the task with a sizeable bonus if I succeeded and nothing other than my salary if I did not.

I had performed similar services for them in the past so they were hopeful. I also had my eye on a yacht that Patricia and I loved. Therefore, I was well motivated.

I joined the company and commenced my task by thoroughly reviewing the existing contracts, visiting every customer (regardless of size) in the local area. I set up phone calls with most customers that were far away with the intent of visiting them as time permitted.

I had a conference call with the client in question. I am going call them XYZ Telecom for the purpose of this book. My reasons will become apparent to you later in this narration. During the conference call, I spoke with a Mr. Rob Welsh the Director of Operations for XYZ telecom.

I introduced myself made small talk and asked him the customary question of his satisfaction with the project and the onsite personnel. His response was very positive. He indicated that he was very satisfied with the status of the project and the progress to date.

The yearlong project was only six weeks from completion. Therefore, I gave it no further thought.

Therefore, I was very surprised when I got the phone call. It was about 6:15 AM on a Friday in September. I was just leaving my house to head into work. My cell phone rang. When I answered it,

Pete, the onsite project manager at the client site in San Marcos, TX, informed me that XYZ Telecom had barred the project team from setting foot on the client premises and were threatening to sue.

I told him that I would be down in San Marcos, Texas on the first flight I could find. Instead of driving to the office, I drove to Washington Dulles Airport. Along the way, I called my EA and asked her to book me on a flight to Austin, TX and arrange for a rental car when I got there.

Luckily, there was a seat available on a flight leaving Dulles at 7:25 AM. In the pre 9-11 era, one could just get a last minute ticket and still make a flight as long as you got to the airport thirty minutes prior to flight time. I do miss those days.

To make a long story short, I landed in Austin at about 11:00 AM Central time. I was famished. I do not like airline food. Therefore, I had not had anything to eat. However, I did not stop for anything.

I picked up the rental car and arrived at the offices of XYZ telecom at about 11:45 AM. I walked in to the building and asked the receptionist for Mr. Rob Welsh. Before she could call his office, he walked by. He was en-route from the call-center to his office. She hailed him and I introduced myself.

His first words were not hello, or good morning. He did not take my outstretched hand. Instead, he said, "I thought I told all you assholes to not set foot on my premises."

I replied, "I am sorry Mr. Welsh, I thought you meant the other assholes from my company."

"I just flew in from DC."

The big burly Texan paused. I saw a hint of a smile. He then said, "You are not going to convince me of anything, you guys conned me."

"I am going to sue your company."

"I am not going to pay you a dime and I want you people gone."

"I will never do business with you again."

"I do not even want to talk business with you."

I let him finish venting and then said, "Mr. Welsh, like I said, I just flew here from DC. I have not eaten anything since I woke up."

"Can I buy you lunch if I promise not to talk about business."

He hesitated for almost fifteen seconds and then said, "If you say even one word about business, I will walk out."

"I am going to have lunch with you Atul and I will buy."

"I am not happy with your company but I am not inhospitable."

"You are in my town; I have not forgotten my manners."

I nodded in agreement. He then asked me if I would like to use the facilities while he retrieved his suit jacket. I thanked him.

When he came back down, he said, "It is better if I drive, since I know the area and you don't."

I thanked him again.

He then asked me what kind of food I liked.

"Mr. Welsh," I said, "I am so hungry I could eat a horse."

He asked me if I liked hot-spicy food. I replied in the affirmative. I think I actually said something to the effect that spicy food was my favorite kind.

"Great," he said, "I know just the place."

He took me to a Tex-Mex place. We ordered our drinks and we started talking about hot sauce. He went over the menu, told me about his favorite dishes, and made some recommendations.

He also told me that most dishes were available in several grades of spiciness ranging from mild to volcano.

He asked me how I liked my food. "Volcano, of course" I replied.

"Good man." Rob said. He ordered for both of us and asked me if I had tasted 'Hellfire' sauces. I said I had but I preferred 'Deathwish' and 'El Yucateco' habanero sauces to 'Hellfire'.

I am not claiming that any one of these is better. It is just my personal preference. We then began discussing the quality, taste and other pros and cons of these hot sauces. Then we discussed our many experiences with spicy foods (both good and bad). I felt that I was developing a rapport with Rob.

Let me tell you something folks. The temptation to talk about business at that moment was by far one of the worst temptations I have experienced in my life. It took a considerable amount of will power and the Grace of God to keep me from mentioning work. I got through lunch without mentioning a single word of business.

When Rob drove me back to his office, I thanked him for the food. He then asked me what my plans were.

I said, "Rob, you do not wish to discuss business. I have given you my word to that effect."

"So, I will just drive back to the airport and see if I can find a flight back to DC."

"However, I really enjoyed the lunch." I continued. "My whole mouth feels like it is on fire."

"Yeah great isn't it." He said. "Well Atul you are truly a man of your word."

"I cannot understand how you managed to get through lunch without talking about business."

"By the way, you will not make the last flight back to DC. It leaves at 3:00PM."

"You better check into the LaQuinta Inn."

"I will have my secretary call in the reservation."

I thanked him again. To which he commented. "Since you have time to kill, come into my office let me tell you what is going on."

He then proceeded to tell me that my project manager Pete had not been truthful on the project status reports. Rob was now sure that we would not make the delivery date. I asked Rob for about thirty minutes to investigate exactly what was going on and then promised to report to him.

I also asked for use of a conference room where I could speak to my project team. He obliged. I called my Project Manager on his cell phone and asked him to assemble the project team in the XYZ Telecom conference room.

It took them about fifteen minutes to get there. They had all gone back to their respective rooms at the LaQuinta Inn. I later found out that this was the only hotel within driving distance. When the team assembled, I asked them to tell me what was going on.

The lead engineer (Amir) and project manager (Pete) started talking simultaneously. I then remembered Rob's words about the status reports.

I raised my hand halted the conversation and said. "Before we proceed, Pete, please tell me if your project reports were accurate."

"Specifically, when did you know that we had a schedule problem?"

He started telling me about how he was sure we could make up the schedule and why that justified the way he reported on schedule performance in the project reports, blah, blah, blah.....

I stopped him mid-sentence and asked him if he remembered the first meeting I had with the professional services management staff when I joined the company.

I said, "I distinctly remember saying, under no condition do we lie to or mislead the client."

Without much ado, I dismissed him effective immediately, and asked him to go to our office in DC on Monday to have HR formalize the paperwork.

I also instructed him to leave the client site.

I then asked Amir, the lead engineer, to explain the situation to me. Here is what I gathered from Amir's narrative.

We were delivering a new call center solution to XYZ telecom. Everything from a new phone-switch (which is actually as big as a room), to new client-server based systems to replace the old mainframe systems.

Apparently, the new telephone switch was on the bleeding edge of technology and still had a few bugs. The phone-switch was supposed to talk to the servers by means of "events". Do not ask me what 'events' mean in this technical context. I do not know and I do not want to know.

Somehow, the event triggered by a call hang up was not being transmitted from the phone-switch to the server. Therefore, if a caller hung up before the Call Center Representative (CCR), this caused the call-guide software on CCR's PC to malfunction and freeze. At that time, the only option was to shut down and restart the software.

Amir also informed me that the phone-switch manufacturer was aware of the problem and was working on a bug fix. Unfortunately, the fix would not be available in time for the delivery date. Therefore, it appeared that the only share of the blame that we as a company had was the fact that my project manager had lied on his status reports.

I went back to Rob as promised and explained the situation to him taking care NOT TO emphasize the fact that the problem was actually the phone-switch manufacturer.

I then asked Rob why the delivery date was so critical. I said, "This is a fixed price contract, if we go over by a week or so, you do not get charged extra."

"That's not the point." He said, "It is the press."

He then proceeded to tell me that the executives at XYZ Telecom had arranged for a big press affair. It was scheduled for two days after our promised delivery date. Representatives from the local TV and several newspapers were expected to attend.

I listened carefully to what Rob had to say and then asked him the following.

"Rob, if I understand you correctly, it is imperative to have a successful press affair regardless of if the system working flawlessly. Is this correct?"

His answer was exactly what I expected. "Atul, if the press event does not go well, I will lose my job."

I then said, "I do not want to give you false hope."

"However, if I my engineers figure out a way to make the systems be stable on the day of the press event, and ensure a successful demonstration for the press, would this keep your executives happy."

He said that he was certain it would. I gathered more details from him about the press event and found out that it was scheduled for about forty-five minutes and organized as follows:

- Fifteen minutes of briefings
- Fifteen minutes of demonstration
- Fifteen minutes of questions and answers

I took Rob's leave to go back and talk to the team. I also called my wife and informed her that I would not be home that night.

I asked Amir if there was a way to stabilize the system for at least fifteen minutes. He answered that he could not guarantee the stability if the caller hung up first.

However, he demonstrated the system to me and showed me that all the CSR had to do was hang up before the caller and the system worked fine.

Amir also showed me the steps involved in restarting the call guide program should the caller hang up first. Amir also informed me that there was only one aisle in the call center where TV crews and press members could walk through unobstructed.

After about twenty minutes of conversations, Amir and I had the rudiments of a workable plan that we would implement over the next five days in time for the press event. Here it is:

- We were going to ask Rob to seat twenty of his best CSR's in the center aisle.
- We were going to get one of our trainers to train the twenty CSR to hang up on callers just as they said goodbye.
- We were also going to train them to restart the program gracefully should any caller

beat them to the hang up event. and

♦ We were going to pray hard that this plan worked.

I went back to Rob's office with Amir in tow and told him what we had planned. Rob was interested. However, he had one additional request. He wanted me to be onsite to ensure that everything would go well for the press event which was scheduled for the following Thursday.

I informed him that I had to go back to DC the next day (Saturday). However, I assured him that I would be back Monday morning and would plan to stay through Friday.

He said, "Atul, I need you to give me your word that you will see this through."

As soon as he said those words, I knew that I had achieved a trusted relationship with Rob.

Well let us just say that the plan worked and the press event was a resounding success. Rob was busy all day on Thursday, first with the press and then with the XYZ Telecom executives. I did not see much of him that day.

I went to Rob's office on Friday to let him know that I was heading back. I also had news that the bug fix from the telephone-switch manufacturer had arrived and my team would complete the project within eight to ten days.

Rob told me that he had informed his bosses about the excellent job we had done. It seems he left out the part about the glitches and crisis of the week prior. I thanked him again and hoped I would see him sometime soon.

To which Rob replied, "Well Atul, you will really like the restaurant that I take you to next month when you come back to sign the contract for modernizing our San Antonio call center."

That contract proved to be worth eight million dollars. Rob has since become a good friend and we correspond on a regular basis. We still alert each other via email as soon as we find a new or unique hot sauce.

I wish I could say that I succeeded in resolving all the issues at that company, got my big bonus and bought that yacht.

Alas! It was not to be.

By the third board meeting, I had to inform my venture capitalist friends that this company would take at least three years to fix.

They did not want to let their investment ride for that long. Therefore, they sold the company to another venture capitalist company, and recovered their cost.

I went on to other things.

Let us examine my interactions with Rob a little closer. When I first arrived, I let him talk and I LISTENED. I did not try to defend, sell, act outraged or anything of the sort.

Please note that I was in this listening mode from the time I arrived, through lunch, until Rob decided to talk about business and relayed the situation to me.

Then I demonstrated a thorough UNDERSTANDING of his problem by empathizing with the fact that he could potentially be fired if the press event did not go well.

Next, I achieved his buy in by SOLICITING his input on whether the press event was more important than the actual flawless functioning of the system.

I then provided Rob with TRUSTED ADVICE by working out a plan for achieving a successful press demonstration.

Also, take note that I established commonality with him through our mutual love for hot sauce and spicy food. I did not force this interaction. I did not pretend to like hot sauce.

Some of you might say that this was very easy because Rob and I liked hot sauce.

What if Rob did not like hot sauce?

Let me assure you that if you truly listen to someone and really hear what he or she is saying, ninety-nine percent of the time you will find that you have something in common with him or her.

Also, remember if there was nothing else that Rob and I had in common, we both had inherent commonality in the fact that we both needed this project to succeed, each for our own reasons. This would have been commonality enough.

Although this is not a frequent occurrence in my career, I have had one or two interactions where the only thing my client and I discussed was the project at hand.

Chapter Eight
Criteria Based Decision Making

I have to discuss criteria based decision making in conjunction with the LUST technique.

There are many occasions where after applying the LUST technique, the client expects you to help them with making a decision or decisions that will help alleviate the problem at hand.

While it feels great to be able to offer your own personal advice on the matter, this is actually a stage where you need to separate yourself from the decision. I am not suggesting that you abandon your client. I am merely emphasizing that if you make the decision for the client, it will always be your decision and they may never fully take ownership.

The problem with giving the client a solution without involving them is that somewhere along the line they may feel that they were being sold. Remember: People like to buy. People do not like being sold or being forced to buy.

Therefore, how do you help your client make a decision while ensuring that they maintain ownership for the decision?

I have detailed two simple techniques below.

- ♦ Linear Analysis Technique, and
- ♦ The "So What" Analysis technique sometimes known as the "Leads To" Analysis technique

Linear Analysis Technique:

When you are following this process, you lead your client through an analysis and decomposition of the problem starting with the problem and working your way down to possible solutions and their ramifications. This is essentially a top down approach.

The structure of this exercise should be as follows:

Background: The first step is to work with the client to describe the background, result or utopian state that they hope to achieve.

Problem: The second step is to work with the client to identify the problems or obstacles that are preventing them from achieving the desired results.

Corrective actions: The third step is to work with the client to identify potential corrective actions that they could take to mitigate the problem or problems identified above.

Ramifications: The fourth step is to work with the client to identify the effects of each corrective action, both positive and negative.

Decision: The final step is to identify the

corrective action or group of actions that help in achieving the desired results with minimum negative impact.

Example:

Background: The nation's border is exposed.
Problem: Congress has asked me to safeguard the border against terrorists entering our country. What can I do to protect the border?

Corrective Actions:

a. I could station guards at frequent intervals.
b. I could put up miles of fencing.

Ramifications:

Ramifications of (a). In order to be effective the guards will have to be spaced not too far apart. This will require many guards. This is a high recurring expense.
Ramifications of (b). A contractor needs to be hired to put up the fences. The fences may not cover the entire border.

Decision:

The potential solution is most probably a combination of (a) and (b).

The "So What" Analysis Technique:

This is essentially a bottom up approach. When you are following this process, you lead your client through an analysis and decomposition of the problem starting with the possible solution/s and working out the impacts that they will have towards achieving the stated goal.

The reason this technique is known as the "So What" technique is that you literally ask the question "so what" at each stage until you arrive at the final outcome.

The structure of this exercise should be as follows:

Statement of Goal/s: The first step is to work with the client to describe the result that they hope to achieve.

Inputs: The second step is to work with the client to identify the potential solutions that they feel will help them achieve the desired goal.

Outputs: The third step is to work with the client to identify potential process impacts that each solution will produce.

Outcomes: The final step is to identify the outcome/s that will result from the proposed inputs and their resulting outputs.

Example:

Statement of Goals: The border is not adequately protected. I have been tasked with safeguarding the border against terrorism

Potential Inputs:

I could do so by using fences (scenario1) or by adding guards (scenario2)

Scenario 1

I put up miles of fences. - (Input)

[So what?]

This will make it harder for individuals that are trying to get across the border illegally. - (Output)

[So what?]

They will either try to get in legally or try to get in at another spot. - (Output)

[So what?]

If I put up enough fences, I will be able to protect the border and reduce illegal immigration. - (Outcome)

Scenario 2

I station guards at regular intervals. - (Input)

[So what?]

The guards will identify individuals trying to enter the border illegally and stop them. - (Output)

[So what?]

They will either try to get in legally or try to get in at another spot. - (Output)

[So what?]

If I station enough guards, I will be able to protect the border and make it difficult for terrorists to cross the border illegally. - (Outcome)

Decision - (Based on scenario 1 & scenario 2): Therefore, the potential solutions are to station enough guards or put up enough fences or a combination of the two.

Both techniques are equally effective with respect to their help in arriving at proposed course of action. I do not particularly recommend one over the other. I have used both techniques quite effectively. Personally, I let the client's style influence my choice of technique.

Your choice of technique should depend on your personal comfort and familiarity with the technique while giving consideration to your client's preferences and their thought patterns or their decision-making abilities.

Some individuals are very adept of thinking in a top down manner while others are more comfortable using the bottom up approach.

I strongly recommend that you study both techniques and apply it to day-to-day situations in your personal life until you are thoroughly familiar and fully comfortable with both techniques.

I am aware that the example I used above makes it appear as if I am trivializing a serious problem. I am not. I used the above example to depict that these analysis techniques are viable options for initial solution ideas regardless of the size of the problem.

Now let us try both these techniques on a business problem.

Linear Analysis Technique:

Business Example:

Background: My Company is installing a new CRM system. The company executives have scheduled a press conference with the local press and TV stations for two weeks from today.

Problem: The system is not working as desired and has some critical bugs. There appears to be no way to make the system fully functional on or before the date of the press conference. What can I do to make the press conference successful?

Corrective Actions:

a. I could fire the subcontractor performing the work and cancel the press conference.

b. I could work with the contractor and figure out a stopgap method to highlight the areas of the system that are currently functional for the purposes of the press conference. I can worry about total bug fixing later.

Ramifications:

Ramifications of (a). Regardless of whether I blame/fire the contractor, the fallout of canceling the press conference will be high. The company executives will not look on my performance favorably.

Ramifications of (b). Since the contractor is willing to work with me to highlight the fully functional areas of the system for the press conference, there is a high probability that the press conference will be a success. There is still some risk.

Decision: Solution (a) is not a good solution. My best recourse is to select solution (b).

The "So What" Analysis Technique:

Business Example:

Statement of Goals: My Company is installing a new CRM system. The Company executives have scheduled a press conference with the local press and TV stations for two weeks from today. We have identified critical bugs in the system that cannot be fixed prior to the press conference. I have to mitigate the risk and take action prior to the press conference.

Potential Inputs:

I could mitigate risk by firing the subcontractor performing the work and canceling the press conference (scenario1) or by working with the contractor and figuring out a stopgap method to highlight the areas of the system that are currently functional for the purposes of the press conference. (scenario2)

Scenario 1

I fire the subcontractor performing the work and cancel the press conference. - (Input)

[So what?]

This may potentially shift the blame for the cancellation squarely on the subcontractor performing the work. - (Output)

[So what?]

However, my executives may or may not take kindly to the cancellation of the press conference. - (Output)

[So what?]

I might end up sharing the blame for the botched job anyway. - (Outcome)

Scenario 2

I work with the contractor and figure out a stopgap method to highlight the areas of the system that are currently functional for the purposes of the press conference. - (Input)

[So what?]

The chances are high that the press will focus on the highlighted areas and give us good reviews. - (Output)

[So what?]

This will result in a successful press conference and make the executives happy. - (Output)

[So what?]

I would have mitigated the risk, had a successful press conference and now I can worry about getting the bugs fixed without the press conference hanging over my head. - (Outcome)

Decision - (Based on scenario 1 & scenario 2): Scenario 1 does not seem to be a viable scenario. I have to choose scenario 2.

If this example sounds familiar to you, it should. Think back to the last chapter and the Rob Welsh situation. I used this technique throughout my interaction with Rob to help him make the decision. I did not actually sit down with a piece of paper and follow the steps above. I just talked him through the steps.

Please remember that the process for following these steps in the Rob Welsh scenario took me almost a whole day. There is no time limit on this exercise. You do not have to force the client to a decision. So do not sit there with a pencil and paper and tell the client. "Here I have got the perfect solution for you."

Always remember that you have to lead and suggest. The client needs to make and own the decision. I am going to repeat myself once more. People like to buy. People do not like being sold. This does not apply exclusively to tangible goods. It also applies to intangibles like ideas, decisions etc.

Chapter Nine
Three Principles

People have often asked me what some of the things are that they can do to avoid unexpected surprises and/or situations.

Unfortunately, there is really nothing you can do to avoid surprise situations. Folks, I stress again, we live in an every changing world. The only constant is change. Therefore, things change all the time.

Sometimes the rate of change can be so rapid that some scenario that you thoroughly prepared for prior to a client meeting may change in the time it takes you to commute from your office to the client site.

There are other times that you client is going to request something from you that requires you to make decisions that you know will anger and or irritate your bosses.

At the same time, the client may be so important that you have to make the decision. This situation will arise so you need to be prepared.

There are however, a few principles that you can follow that will help you effectively deal with these situations as and when they arise.

I can sum up these three principles in the following words.

- ◆ Be prepared but also be flexible.
- ◆ Expound on the virtues of your company's capabilities and/or products, however, do not fall prey to your own bull.
- ◆ Play within the guidelines but also know when to step out of the box

I have three really wild stories that depict these situations. However, I reserve those stories for my seminars. Here are the next best examples that help emphasize these scenarios.

<u>Be prepared but also be flexible:</u> One of my Account Executives (Andy) had been beating down the door of a large healthcare provider for several months. Let us call them ABC Healthcare.

Over the past year, Andy had established a strong trusted relationship with the Vice President of ABC Healthcare (Ms. Janet Liu).

One day, Andy called me and said, "Atul, I think we are ready to sign a deal with ABC Healthcare for a large call-center modernization."

"My contact Janet is setting up a meeting with their COO (Stu) to ink the deal." Andy continued.

"Can you be available to fly to San Francisco at short notice?"

My response was, "Andy, for that client, you just call and I will be on a plane."

Andy's call came a week later. He called me on a Monday and informed me that ABC Healthcare had a board meeting that Tuesday.

The COO (Stu) was going to get approval for the call-center modernization at that meeting. Janet (Client, VP) had scheduled a meeting between Andy, Janet, Stu and me for Wednesday. Presumably to review and sign the contract.

I had my EA (executive assistant) make appropriate flight reservations and flew to San Francisco on Tuesday evening.

Andy met me at my hotel on Wednesday morning at 8:00 AM and we drove to the offices of ABC Healthcare.

Andy had already sent me some background material on ABC Healthcare and some very detailed notes on his conversations to date. I made certain that I read the information he sent me thoroughly. Therefore, I was well prepared to discuss the deal and our Company's call center modernization capabilities with the folks at ABC Healthcare, should the need arise.

I was expecting a smooth sailing all the way. I could not have been further from the reality.

When we arrived at ABC Healthcare, we were ushered to the conference room and offered beverages, etc. A few minutes later, Janet and Stu made their entrance.

After introductions, Stu said. "Well there is no point beating around the bush. Let me get directly to the point."

If there were any words that could create a sinking feeling in the pit of your stomach in similar circumstances, these would be them.

"Gentlemen," Stu continued, "I know that you came here expecting to sign a contract for call center modernization."

"However, the board has decided that our provider portal is woefully lacking and is the highest priority item for us."

He went on to describe how the Board sometimes forces their hand and how operations had to adjust their plans accordingly. I will not bore you with the rest of Stu's monologue.

Stu concluded. "We will of course reimburse you, Dr. Uchil, for your flight and trip expenses."

Andy turned ashen. Stu and Janet seemed visibly embarrassed.

It took me almost a whole minute to recover.

I said, "Stu, first of all let me thank you for your candor."

"I have been on the receiving end of Board decisions and dealt with the burden of having to deliver this information to employees and clients." I continued. "It is never easy."

"However, since I am here Stu, may I ask you to tell me about your portal issues?"

Stu said, "I can fill you in." "No problem there." "Do you guys' sell portals also?"

"Stu we offer a broad range of consulting services." I said.

"No, we do not sell portal per se." I continued. "To the best of my knowledge, the two leading portal solutions out there are offered by Microsoft and Oracle"

"However, we have helped implement both of these technologies at several commercial and Federal clients."

"Being technology agnostic, we have also helped our clients decide which technology is best suited for their need without being biased."

"We have also helped many clients identify requirements and customize portals to best suit their needs." I said.

I then asked the following "Has the board set any deadline for the portal?"

Stu said, "Yes, they want us to identify a solution within three months and complete implementation within a period of six to nine months after the solution is identified."

My next question was, "How are you planning to select and implement the replacement for your portal?"

"I am not quite sure." Stu said. "Our IT department is woefully understaffed."

"I guess we would have to bring in a consultant such as you to get this accomplished."

This was my cue.

I said, "Stu, you and Janet trusted us to modernize your call center." "You were planning to execute a contract with us today."

"While my technology staff will change, Andy will still be your primary contact."

"Further, you know our rates are competitive and we could get ramped up within a week"

Stu paused for a few seconds and then said, "I was already thinking along those lines."

"It would certainly save us time." He added.

He concluded with the following, "However, I can only sign you up for the upfront three-month evaluation and selection if your price is right."

"Stu, if you give us thirty minutes, Andy and I will make a call back east."

"Andy and I will consult with the technical folks and have a quote for you."

To make a long story short, we inked a deal for the evaluation that very same day.

That was not all, Andy continued building the trusted relationship with Janet and Stu and our technical team did a great job on the evaluation process.

As a result, we were also awarded the portal build out. It did not stop there, it took almost a year, and then we were awarded the call-center modernization contract.

I do not recall the numbers exactly but ABC Healthcare proved to be about a fifty million dollar client over the period of four years.

I am going to ask you to think carefully about this interaction for a minute.

Did it sound familiar to you?

You are getting it, just think LUST in action.

I always tend to fallback on the Lust technique when I am faced with unexpected situations.

<u>Expound on the virtues of your company's capabilities and/or products, however, do not fall prey to your own bull:</u> This is common sense folks.

You always put the best face of your company forward when talking about the company.

No one (especially your client) wants to hear about the woes or troubles that are inherent in every organization.

However, the caution here is never to fall prey to the hype especially while making promises to clients or vendors etc.

For example if the client asks you about your company's, project delivery capabilities.

I would answer that question by saying. "Mr. or Ms. Client, we have some of the best qualified professional services personnel and engineers working for us."

"We always strive for one hundred percent on schedule project completion."

"In addition, we have a very high success rate of delivering projects on schedule."

"However, there are unavoidable circumstances that occur from time to time, that prevent on schedule project completion for some clients."

"We will strive to mitigate any risks that may arise to ensure that we deliver your project on time."

Yes! There is a lot of hype in the above statements. However, you have qualified it at the end with the part about unavoidable circumstances and risk mitigation.

Is this lying to the client? No, it is not. You have told them that while you strive for perfection, you sometimes fall short.

Some people have asked me is the hype necessary?

I feel that it is always necessary to put your best face forward. As long as you take care not to cross the line between putting your best face forward and lying.

How do you think your client would feel if you answered the delivery capabilities question in the following manner?

"Well when we did XYZ project, the project manager quit halfway. It took our HR two weeks to find a replacement. As a result, the project was delayed."

"Then when we did the ABC project, our engineers ended up being double booked. Someone in scheduling messed-up. As a result that project was delayed."

"However, we delivered almost all the rest of our projects on schedule and within budget."

Essentially, you have conveyed the same information that I conveyed above with one exception. You said it all in a very negative manner. Will this invoke confidence in the client?

NO!

Please always put your best face forward. Nevertheless, remember that under no circumstances should you lie or mislead the client.

My Grandma once told me a fable about a king who had a dream that all his teeth fell out except one. He called his soothsayer and asked him to interpret the dream.

The soothsayer said, "Your majesty this is a bad omen."

"It means that all your relatives will die before you."

What was the king's reaction? My grandma said it was something like "Off with is head…"

Then the king called in another soothsayer and recounted the dream to him. This soothsayer was not only knowledgeable; he was also wise as to the method of delivering messages.

He said, "your majesty this is cause for celebration.'

"This means that you will have a very long life."

"In fact you will live the longest amongst all your relatives."

The king showered him with riches and land etc.

The point here is that both soothsayers essentially delivered the same message. What was different was the mode of delivery.

I know in a previous chapter, I have asked you not to put a spin on bad news to the client. However, in this case, the news is not necessarily bad. It is just neutral news. However, a negative spin makes it appear bad.

I hope I was able to make the difference clear to you.

In short, be positive.

<u>Play within the guidelines but know when to step out of the box:</u> Every company has written and unwritten guidelines setup for you to follow. I call these the sandbox.

On occasion, you will come across a situation

where you have to step outside the sandbox for a special client. Do not make it a habit, but make appropriate exceptions as necessary. Remember nothing is written in stone.

Here is an example: We were doing business with this large healthcare client. Yes, it is ABC Healthcare, the same one I mentioned before. After we were done with their portal work, we started on their call center modernization.

They proved to be a ten million dollars per year client for us. One day, about two and a half years into our relationship with ABC Healthcare, my account executive Andy called me and said, "We have a problem."

"With ABC Healthcare?" I asked.

"Yes Atul, they want us to modify our base call guide software and add ….."

Let me stop here and tell you that it was our company policy (very strictly enforced) not to modify core software for any single client. The Board of Directors felt (and rightfully so) that if we did this for one client, every client would want modifications. As a result, we would never have base software.

The policy was that when a client requested modifications that could not be handled by tailoring, we took note and informed the client that we would incorporate the changes in the next release of the software.

Since ABC Healthcare was such a good client, I asked Andy to tell them that we needed a couple of days to study their request.

I then called in our technical experts and asked them to evaluate what it would take to accommodate ABC Healthcare's request and put out a patch release.

Armed with the information provided to me by the technical experts, I performed a cost benefit analysis and ran it up to the CEO. He blessed it and I authorized the work.

I then made the trip out to the West Coast and met with Stu and Janet. I informed them of the policy and told them that we were making an exception for them. I also showed them the cost involved with the effort.

Not surprisingly, Stu stepped in and offered to cover the development costs. Every one was happy. Not everyone actually!

Well let me tell you, that both the CEO and COO (me) got our asses chewed out at the next Board meeting. We were informed that the reason the Board setup policies were for the betterment of the company, etc., etc, etc.

Then the Board looked at the P&L and wondered why there was a drop in development costs even though we put out a patch release.

I gleefully informed them that we had got the client to pay for the patch even though it would be incorporated into our next full version release as standard functionality.

This appeased them some and subsequently they made a change to the policy saying that if a client offered to pay the development costs for a patch that would end up being part of a subsequent version release, then we could accept such client requests.

Did I know that I was going to be chewed out by the Board? Of course I did. Did the CEO know that he was going to be chewed out by the Board? Of course he did.

Was I going to go back to a client that had generated twenty million in revenue over the past two years and tell them that I could not help them because of some policy? Hell No!

The point I am trying to get across is that sometimes you will be in a situation wherein you have to make decisions that take you outside the sandbox and take the heat for them.

As long as you are making these decisions in good faith with both the Client and your Company's best interests, you will come out a hero.

This does not mean that you will not take heat along the way. So be prepared.

I will end this chapter by reiterating:

- ♦ Be prepared but also be flexible.
- ♦ Expound on the virtues of your company's capabilities and/or products, however, do not fall prey to your own bull.
- ♦ Play within the guidelines but also know when to step out of the box

Chapter Ten
Achieving Consistent Success

What is consistent success? Forget about the corporate world. Let us talk about consistent success in a generalized context.

During a career spanning nine years, Bjorn Borg won forty-one percent of the Grand Slam Singles tournaments that he entered and over eighty-nine percent of the Grand Slam singles matches that he played.

Would you have considered Bjorn Borg great just because he won one Wimbledon title?

Cal Ripken played a record two thousand six hundred and thirty-two consecutive games spanning sixteen seasons from 1982 through 1998.

Would everyone call Cal Ripken the great "iron man of baseball" if he played ten consecutive games or even a hundred?

Anyone can have a good season, good year or few good years. In a corporate context, anyone can win one large contract, or one big client. Consistent success is what you build over a career.

When I talk about consistent success, I am talking of success over a period of a decade or greater.

Let us talk about kissing the Blarney Stone:

I have always possessed the ability to be eloquent and charming when I wanted. I worked my natural charm on that sales floor at Radio Shack. They used to say back home that I had kissed the Blarney Stone one time too many.

For those of you that are unaware, five miles northwest of the small city of Cork is the village of Blarney. Near the village, standing almost ninety feet high is the castle of Blarney. Cormac MacCarthy erected the present castle in 1446. This is the third castle constructed at that site.

Built on a rock, above several caves, the tower originally had three floors. On the top floor, just below the battlements on the parapet, is the world famous Blarney Stone. This stone supposedly gives the gift of eloquence to all who kiss it. I do not know how long this custom has been practiced or how it originated.

You are probably wondering if I have gone insane. You are also probably asking yourself what relevance the blarney stone has to achieving consistent success.

Let me tell you why I am talking about the Blarney stone. Over the years, people have attributed my success to many factors.

- ♦ Some attribute it to the gift of gab.
- ♦ Others attribute it to my ability to describe things in a manner that everyone understands.

♦ Still others attribute it to other traits both physical and mental.

I am not going to delve very deeply into personal success factors in this book. Many good books out there address this topic in detail. However, I would like to share a few ideas about success that I have formulated through my observations over the years.

I have met and interacted with successful people from all walks of life. Some of them are very intelligent, some are outgoing, some have the gift of gab, some have dynamic personalities, some are charming, some are technically talented, some are great managers, etc.

What is the common theme here? In all honesty folks, there seems to be none. However, I have noticed several traits that consistently successful people share.

They are ethical. Successful people exhibit a core set of personal and professional ethics and honesty that they are not willing to compromise.

They exhibit perseverance. They are willing to work through the hard times and strive towards the desired goal. They do not give up at the first sign of trouble or hardship. Tough times do not last, tough people do.

They have a good work life balance. They work hard and play hard. They are able to separate their work life from their personal life and give both the appropriate attention. Contrary to what most people think work-life balance is not always at the same fifty-fifty level. Sometimes you have a crunch time at work and have to put your family on the back burner for a week or so. At other times, you have to put your work on the back burner and devote more time to your family. If someone tells me that every week is a crisis at work and that he or she cannot find family time, I advise him or her to find another job.

They are multi-dimensional. They are successful in more than one area. For example, they are excellent managers and they coach their kid's baseball team. Alternatively, they are great programmers and a key participant at the local non-profit.

Last but not the least they practice. Whenever they learn something new or need to use some new tool, technique or trait, they deliberately practice it until it becomes second nature. To that end, they are always learning.

One last thought I would like to leave you with here is that we live in an ever-changing world. What you know today may be obsolete next year. You have to persevere, you have to adapt, you have to learn constantly and you have to practice what you have learned in order to be consistently successful.

Chapter Eleven

Selling You

This chapter is for those diehards that still believe relationship selling is not for them. If you think carefully, your career is a series of selling events. This applies whether you are an engineer, programmer, manager, accountant, secretary or whatever else you call yourself. Moreover, the commodity that you are selling is the most important item that you will ever sell.

Think about it. You constantly have to sell yourself, your skills and your capabilities. This process does not occur just during interviews. It is an ongoing day-to-day process.

What would happen if your boss began to doubt your ability to perform six-months into your job?

Would you still have that job?

Alternatively, will the boss terminate your services regardless of how well you did in your interview?

I do not have to tell you, you already know the answer to that question.

I have often heard the expression, "An ounce of image is worth a pound of performance."

This statement is very true in every sense of the word. I have experienced this from both ends of the spectrum, vis-à-vis, the attitude of my bosses towards me and my attitude towards my employees.

Let us examine this scenario. My employee 'Bob' has taken the time and effort to develop a relationship with me. As a result, I trust Bob. In addition, I believe that Bob is a strong performer and a definite go-getter. Bob has displayed a steady performance in the past.

One Thursday afternoon, I see Bob walking into a restaurant. What is the first thought that goes through my mind? Let me tell you.

I think, "Bob is probably meeting with a client or potential client."

On the other hand, my employee 'Tim' has not taken the time and effort to develop a relationship with me. As a result, I am not sure quite what to make of Tim. Tim has displayed a similar performance to Bob.

However, in the back of my mind I am not completely at ease with Tim, despite his performance. One Thursday afternoon, I see Tim walking into a restaurant. What is the first thought that goes through my mind? Let me tell you.

I think the following, "I wonder if Tim is goofing off. What is he doing in a restaurant on a Thursday afternoon instead of being at the office?"

Some of you may think that I am being unfair to Tim and not giving him a fair chance. You are absolutely correct. Logically speaking, Tim and

Bob have the same probability of either meeting with a client or goofing off.

In an ideal world, we would all make decisions based purely on logic. However, I am not here to describe utopia to you. If we all made decisions purely on logic, we would probably all drive cars that get the best gas mileage regardless of how they looked.

No one would ever buy a Ferrari or Viper knowing that they would never fully utilize even fifty percent the vehicle's capabilities.

Reality-check folks! Guess what! We are humans. We make most decisions in our life based on our emotions. Logic comes a distant second when compared to emotions. When you accept that you are human, your boss is human, your co-workers are human and your employees are human, you will immediately realize the importance of establishing the trusted relationship with all these people.

Once again, I am not saying that you have to be everyone's best friend. That is not possible and more importantly not practical. However, I cannot stress the importance of taking the time and effort to get to know everyone and to get everyone to know and trust you.

Patricia brought to my attention that I mention the word sell in this chapter many times and that it might sound contrary to advice that I have expounded in previous chapters. Let me clarify. When I mention selling here, I am talking about relationship selling. You cannot make someone hire you. You cannot force someone to promote you.

You cannot sell 'you' to people. You have to get people to buy you. Think back to the premise of this book. People like to buy. People do not like being sold or being forced to buy.

I have often heard words to the effect,

- ◆ "John Doe is a natural sales man."
- ◆ "Jane Doe is a born leader."
- ◆ "Larry Doe was born with the programmer gene."
- ◆ "Peter Doe is a natural artist."

Sorry to burst your bubble folks. There is no such thing as natural talent and if there is, it plays an insignificant part in consistent long-term success.

We live in exponential times. Things are changing at an unimaginable rate. What you know today may be obsolete by next year if not sooner.

The primary predicators of success are:

- ◆ Hard work
- ◆ Perseverance
- ◆ Loyalty
- ◆ Honesty
- ◆ Ethics
- ◆ Integrity
- ◆ Willingness to learn and adapt
- ◆ Charisma (the ability to get people to like and trust you)

You will notice that intelligence is conspicuously missing from the list. Intelligence does not ensure consistent long-term success without hard work to back it up.

You could be the smartest person in the world. However, if you are not prone to work hard, you will most likely not achieve success.

You could be the hardest working person in the world. However, if you are not willing to learn and adapt to change, you will most likely not achieve success.

You will notice that I have highlighted "Charisma" in the list above. I have not been able to find the exact description of Charisma.

However, Wikipedia (online) defines at as follows: Charisma refers to a rare trait found in certain human personalities usually including extreme charm and a 'magnetic' quality of personality and/or appearance along with innate and powerfully sophisticated personal communicability and persuasiveness.

When I read this, Charisma to me defines the essence of relationship selling. You have to develop the ability to get people to like you and trust you. You have to develop the ability to establish trusted relationships.

These are learned behaviors that, with enough practice, should become second nature to you and a part and parcel of your personality.

The key ingredients that are necessary include genuineness, respect, sincerity and honesty.

Anticlimax

For those of you that are keeping track: In the introduction to this book, I mentioned the Colonel Wright incident. I mentioned Major Byron Love's post meeting comments. What I did not do was tell you what exactly happened in that meeting.

However, I promised you that I would mention what happened in that meeting later in the book and I guess it is time.

I walked into the Colonel's office and greeted him and I extended by hand.

"Good morning Colonel Wright."

"Thank you for seeing me at such short notice."

Colonel Wright took my outstretched hand, shook it and said, "Thank you Dr. Uchil for being here."

"I know the beltway traffic can be a nightmare at times."

Then he turned to Byron and said, "I guess Dr. Uchil invited you to this meeting."

Byron's response was, "Yes Sir."

Colonel Wright closed his office door, smiled and said, "So Atul, what kind of bad news does it take to make you drive the beltway for an unscheduled meeting with me?"

"Well John." I said, "You are not going to like this."

"David & Eugene resigned this week."

"We are going to have to delay the phase 2 completion by about two weeks or so."

"I am looking for suitable replacements and I will have them here within a week."

Colonel Wright looked me squarely in the eye and said, "Is that it?"

"Yeah, that is it John", I replied.

"Well that's not so bad as long as you are sure we only need a delay of two weeks." John said.

"It might not even be two weeks." I said. "HR thinks they might have an appropriate person identified already."

"I will also ensure that phase 3 has no such issues, John"

"Speaking of Phase 3," John continued, "I have the signed purchase order for you to take back to your contracting folks."

I was going to give it to you next Tuesday but since you are here, one less thing to clutter my desk." He said.

"I apologize again John, and I will have my project manager take steps to ensure that everything is smooth sailing for the rest of the project." I said.

"Speaking of sailing," John said. "Are we still on for this Saturday?"...............

Sounds very anticlimactic does it not? Well it is. Relationship selling is not a series of thrilling events or occurrences. It is the slow and steady building of trust with honesty and integrity.

I had a trusted relationship with Colonel John Wright for over fifteen years. He knew that I would not let him down. He also had faith in the fact that I would have mitigated the risk in advance if this situation were avoidable.

Nothing needed to be said. He trusted that I would come through and I had every intention of coming through.

However, I want to highlight something here. Take note on how I presented the information to Colonel Wright. I did not dramatize it. I did not put a positive or negative spin on it. I just stated the facts, plain and simple.

I also did not try to shield the bad information from Colonel Wright. I let him know as soon as it was practical after I knew.

Any outsider looking in on my meeting with Colonel Wright would ponder, "Atul delivered bad news and walked away with a five-million dollar contract"

"I wonder how he did that."

The outsider has only seen the one meeting. He has not been privy to the years of effort, loyalty, honest, sincerity and consistent delivery it took to achieve that level of trust.

So, I say to this outsider - keep on wondering!!! It is magic!!!

About the Author

Dr. Uchil is an accomplished, results-driven executive with a proven track record of building and growing professional service organizations and demonstrated career success directing complex, multi-million dollar consulting engagements for government and commercial clients. As an imaginative, disciplined, results-oriented leader, he effectively creates teams and processes to reduce costs and drive profitability.

Dr. Uchil has extensive DoD, Civilian-Federal, Commercial, and International experience. Prior to founding Uchil, LLC, Dr. Uchil spent over eighteen years in a variety of senior management roles at several large consulting organizations including Accenture and MCC.

Uchil, LLC offers customized motivational training seminars tailored to the specific needs of the organization and various levels of management (Jr., Mid., Sr., and Exec.) These seminars usually focus on one or more of the following subjects: Management, Leadership, Relationship Selling, Processes and Methodology.

Uchil, LLC also offers business coaching and advice for entrepreneurs and startups. This includes but is not limited to, advice and coaching on management strategy, marketing, sales, financial planning, structuring for profitability, core competency identification and development and plans for growth.

In addition to his PhD in Business Administration, Dr. Uchil also holds an MBA in Consulting Operations Management, a BSEE in Electrical Engineering and a Diploma in Electronics and Telecommunications Engineering. Dr. Uchil's doctoral degree is apostilled by US Secretary of State, General (Ret.) Colin L. Powell and bears his signature and seal.

Dr. Uchil's Certifications and affiliations include but are not limited to the following:

- Lifetime member of the Chartered Institute of Professional Management (CIPM)
- Lifetime member of Armed Forces Communications and Electronics Association (AFCEA)
- Lifetime member of the National Defense Industrial Association (NDIA)
- Member of the Institute of Electrical and Electronics Engineers (IEEE)
- Dr. Uchil serves on the Board of Advisors/Directors for several small/emerging businesses and not-for-profit organizations

Dr. Uchil also serves in the United States Coast Guard Auxiliary as a Senior Staff Officer and is a USCG certified instructor for Public Education and Boating Safety

In addition to many research papers and articles, Dr. Uchil has published several books that are available at Amazon.com, Barnes & Noble, Ingram, Baker & Taylor, Borders, BooksAMillion, Bertram Books UK, Gardners UK, Alibris and many other respected and recognized national and international book retailers.

Dr. Uchil resides in Virginia Beach, VA with his wife Patricia, a talented artist and muralist. They have two grown children a daughter (Lindsey) and a son (Cory).

You can find more information about Uchil, LLC at http://www.uchil-llc.com.

Other Books by the Author

◆ Uchil, A. "The Corporate America Survival Handbook: A Cornucopia of Essential Information" (2005) Outskirts Press, Inc. ISBN: 1598000942

THE CORPORATE AMERICA SURVIVAL HANDBOOK is deliberately narrated in a format that lets the readers go to whatever section they need and read it independently of other sections.

This book is a powerful tool, providing information on a wide variety of topics including, security clearances, the job market, resume writing, patents, trademarks and much more.

This book does not contain any magical formula for success - it is mostly common sense. However, this book gives the reader many invaluable insights into Corporate America that most people do not know.

As the saying goes, "Common sense in an uncommon degree is what the world calls wisdom."

♦ Uchil, A. "Consulting: A Job Or A Lifestyle." (2005) Outskirts Press, Inc. ISBN: 1598000640

CONSULTING: A JOB OR A LIFESTYLE is comprehensive research into the life of persons that choose consulting as a career. It details the pros and cons including the lifestyle sacrifices that are an integral part of consulting.

♦ Uchil, A. "I Opted Out: The Chronicles Of A Rat Race Junkie." (2005) Outskirts Press, Inc. ISBN: 1598000713

I OPTED OUT; narrated in the form of a pseudo-autobiography, takes a poignant and satirical look at the impact of the corporate rat race on the personal life of an individual that is addicted to his work.

Today's society often parades the term 'workaholic' as a catch phrase or a badge of honor. Few recognize that addiction to work can be as dangerous as addiction to drugs or alcohol. The author presents this material in a humorous manner where possible to lighten the burden of reading, while taking care not to let humor dilute the gravity of the message.

CPSIA information can be obtained
at www.ICGtesting.com
Printed in the USA
BVHW03s0225221018
530864BV00001B/34/P